LOST MINES

...OF THE...

GREAT SOUTHWEST

THE MINING JOURNAL

A METAL MINING REVIEW OF THE UNITED STATES AND MEXICO

ESTABLISHED IN 1917

PUBLISHED SEMI-MONTHLY ON THE 15TH AND 30TH

CHARLES F. WILLIS, EDITOR AND PUBLISHER
R. G. MOORE, ASSOCIATE EDITOR

PUBLISHED BY THE
TRADE JOURNAL PUBLISHING CO.
ALSO PUBLISHERS OF
THE BUILDER AND CONTRACTOR

520-528 TITLE AND TRUST BUILDING
PHOENIX, ARIZONA

April 26, 1934

Mr. T. F. Brinegar,
Alamos, Sonora, Mexico

Dear Mr. Brinegar:

I want to thank you for your letter of the 20th and for the news notes which you sent. We hope that we will get similar news from you frequently.

I particularly note your request for a descriptive circular of the book "Lost Mines of the Great Southwest." I am sorry we do not have such a circular.

This book is one compiled by a wealthy old mining man, who has for many years taken a great interest in securing stories of lost mines, and he has made a very considerable effort to trace these stories down just as far as possible to get the original or the most authentic story possible.

He compiled them first as separate stories and was recently induced to put all of these separate stories together into book form. There are probably 60 to 65 separate such mine stories in his book, and they are interestingly told as being the current story, but with no vouching for the authenticity of the original story.

The book sells for $2.00.

Hoping to hear from you often, and with kindest personal regards, I am

Yours very truly,

Charles F. Willis

Publisher,
The Mining Journal

CFW:EB

LOST MINES

...OF THE...

GREAT SOUTHWEST

Including Stories of

HIDDEN TREASURES

By

JOHN D. MITCHELL

The Rio Grande Press, Inc.

GLORIETA, NEW MEXICO · 87535

© COPYRIGHT 1970

THE RIO GRANDE PRESS, INC.,
Glorieta, N. M. 87535

First edition from which this
edition was reproduced
supplied by
International Bookfinders, Inc.,
P. O. Box 3003
Beverly Hills, Calif. 90212

Another first edition loaned
for preparatory use by
David F. Brinegar
Executive Editor
ARIZONA DAILY STAR
Tucson, Ariz.

Photographically enlarged from first
edition in reproduction

A RIO GRANDE CLASSIC
first published in 1933

Library of Congress Card Catalog
70-114964
SBN No. 87380-013-3

First Printing 1970

The Rio Grande Press, Inc.
GLORIETA, NEW MEXICO · 87535

Publisher's Preface

Who doesn't like stories of lost mines and
hidden treasures, especially in lovely Arizona?
It is a delight to go there for any reason, but to go
there to hunt for gold, silver and semi-precious
stones is high adventure even today! The history
of the whole Southwest is alive with legends of
Indian and Spanish treasure, hidden either here
or there. The rugged mountains of fair Arizona
surely hide dozens upon dozens of old mines found
once and then lost forever. It is still fun to go into
that wildly beautiful land seeking lost mines and
hidden treasure; anyone can do it, and someone
can be lucky. Everything you need to know is right
here in this book. It is said that for every ounce
of gold and silver that has been taken from the
land there, tons of it still remains to be discovered. There is no doubt whatsover that this is
utterly and completely true, and when we have
published this book, we're going to take a copy
and go hunting ourselves. Gold was discovered
by accident in California, by accident in Cripple
Creek, and by accident in the Yukon, and we have
often felt that we were accident-prone.

We assure you, in all solemnity, that author Mitchell didn't make these stories up out of thin air. Any reader can find bits and fragments of any or all of these legends throughout the literature of frontier Arizona, and even elsewhere. So, sit down and read *Lost Mines of the Great Southwest, Including Stories of Hidden Treasures,* and then plan a vacation to the finest country in the entire world and hunt yourself a fortune — it's there for the finding, and in this book we tell you how to find it!

Bear in mind, however, that if a greedy federal government doesn't take everything you find in taxes, a greedy state government will (pardon us, Arizona), and if a greedy state government doesn't, a greedy county government will, and if one government or another doesn't get it, inflation will. When you find some treasure, go buy something quick; tomorrow it will cost twice as much.

We wish we could say more about the author of this one book, but we cannot. Our usual sources (Arizona Pioneers' Historical Society, the Phoenix and Tucson Public Libraries, the University of Arizona library, etc.) appear to have nothing in their files, and other repositories of Arizona lore and history yield no information either. Reprinting these old books has caused this to happen to us before; after we release the book, we begin to discover what we wanted to know before we published it. We were unable once to discover anything about Alex Darley, author of our *Passionists of the Southwest, a Revelation of the Penitentes,* but after the book was published and distributed we found a gold mine of information at a public library in a small town in Colorado. Same with James McKenna, who wrote the New Mexico counterpart to this title — *Black Range Tales.* We found a lot of what we needed to know after we published our first printing, and all of what we learned was incorporated into our second edition.

So if we learn something of John D. Mitchell after we release this edition, we will incorporate it into our second edition.

To reprint his title, we acknowledge our

thanks to two good friends. One of them is David Brinegar, Executive Editor of the (Tucson) *Arizona Daily Star*. Dave is a collector of Southwestern books, and one of his treasures is a fine but annotated and penciled copy of the first edition of this title which belonged to his father. When Dave loaned us the book, we found at the back of it a laid-in letter written to his father (then a mining engineer working in Mexico). The letter is reproduced facsimile ahead of these pages, and it tells all we have been able to learn about author Mitchell and this book.

The other friend who came to our aid was Richard (Dick) Mohr of International Bookfinders, Inc., in Beverly Hills, Calif. As he always has on nearly every title we have ever needed, Dick had a first edition handy and loaned it to us. We reprinted from his edition; in reproduction, we photographically enlarged our edition in order to fit it into our standard 6" x 9" format. This helps us old folks with the reading, too, as enlargement makes the type larger. Heaven knows we need it; even billboards have small type these days.

No doubt some of our purist readers will complain about the reproduction of the photographs in this book. To forestall this, if possible, we explain here that the first edition was published in 1933. The original pictures submitted with the manuscript were bad pictures to start with. Then, the original printer appears to have taken very few pains (if any) with the engravings so that the first edition contains poor reproductions of poor pictures. By a technical process, our excellent printer — Walsworth Publishing Co., of Marceline, Mo. — has been able to improve the cuts, and hence, this edition is a far better book mechanically than the first edition was when it was brand new.

This is a beautiful Rio Grande Classic, the 52nd title we have reprinted since we began in 1962. As with all of our titles which need it, we have here added an index. This one was prepared by Miss Katherine McMahon, formerly librarian of the excellent Southwestern collection at the Albuquerque Public Library, Miss McMahon retired from library work the first of this year and took to professional indexing; we are delighted she found the time to do this index for us.

One of our good friends in Santa Fe is Mr. Ron Bayford, an artist, once of London. Ron utilizes a unique and beautiful technique, requiring a steady hand, a keen eye and the very patience of Job. He paints landscapes in ink, developing composition, depth and perspective with nothing but individual dots painstakingly put down one at a time. On the endsheets to this book, front and back, Mr. Bayford has portrayed a lonely rock formation in Arizona. It is scenes like this that hide the secrets of *Lost Mines of the Great Southwest.*

We must acknowledge here, too, our thanks to Mrs. Dorothy Hensley, acquisitions librarian of the Tucson Public Library. Mrs. Hensley has always liked our efforts, and we have imposed on her time and cheerful good nature frequently. She wrote to us last fall, recommending this title; her library copy — the last one — had become so used and mutilated it could no longer be loaned out. We took her suggestion, with thanks. She has recommended some others, too, and in due time, these will also become beautiful Rio Grande Classics.

Negatives of the foldout maps at the front and back of this book were provided by the Arizona Pioneers' Historical Society. We are most grateful for their help and cooperation.

Robert B. McCoy

John T. Strachan

La Casa Escuela,
Glorieta, N. M. 87535

LOST MINES

...OF THE...

GREAT SOUTHWEST

Including Stories of

HIDDEN TREASURES

By

JOHN D. MITCHELL

Press of
THE JOURNAL CO., Inc.
(Rose & Allison)
Phoenix, Arizona
4

INDEX

INDEX—Continued

PREFACE

The search for Lost Mines and Hidden Treasures has ever intrigued mankind and for ages has worn the glamour of legend and romantic mystery. All over the West and Great Southwest rich mineral deposits were found by emigrants and prospectors who could not stop to work them at the time of discovery, or were prevented by hostile Indians from doing so, and in this way they became lost.

Ancient and valuable collections of gold and silver remained buried with the wiping out of the Aztec civilization and later with the passing of the Spanish Conquistadors and the decay and destruction of the early Spanish Missions. Western lore is replete with such incidents, some of which have, no doubt, grown in magnitude of wealth as time elapsed as most traditions do in the extended retrospective until history becomes distorted.

The Toltecs and Aztecs understood the mining and smelting of gold and silver and used it for ornaments with which to adorn themselves and to make shields and household utensils. The great treasures that belonged to the Aztecs and Incas were buried to prevent them from falling into Spanish hands. These great hoards are scattered all over South America and Mexico and all that part of the Great Southwest that belonged to Mexico at the time of the Spanish Conquest.

In many instances the Jesuits established their Missions in the Aztec and Inca mining centers and many rich and valuable mines were opened up and in this way the Spanish took millions from the country.

That the following stories have an authentic background is amply proven by history. The fact that many of the old mines and treasures referred to in the following chapters have not yet been located, has not prevented the author from giving important details as to their value and location. Some parts of the old stories have been omitted in order to present them in a more compact form not possible in the Spanish and Indian languages from which some of them have been translated.

The Author has spent many years on the frontier in Alaska and Old Mexico and in the mountains and on the boundless plains of our own great Southwest. His life has been cast among these old stories when many of the pioneers lived and searched for the lost mines and treasures. He has spent many pleasant hours around the campfires listening to these old stories and the tales and traditions of by-gone days.

It has been truly said that nothing will awaken a white man like the jingle of gold. The search for gold has taken them far into the frozen north to the land of the midnight sun; into the million square miles of equatorial forests and the reptile infested swamps and rivers of South America; across the veldts of darkest Africa; to the Australian Bush; into the wilds of Old Mexico and all over the West and

Great Southwest; down on the Spanish Main with Drake and Riley; to Peru with Pizarro; to Mexico with Cortez, and across the plains with Coronado, in search of the Seven Cities of Cibola.

In memory it takes them back to Treasure Island, back to the Alhambra in Old Granada with its Moorish Castles and secret caves filled with gold and priceless jewels, with Arabian steeds all saddled and bridled and ready to ride.

Many an Anglo-Saxon is a prospector and treasure hunter at heart. To dig up a buried treasure or discover a lost mine is the dream of Eternal Youth. The wonderful thrill of such a discovery cannot, however, be experienced by all of us. Tales of hardships followed by the finding of a fortune in gold dust and nuggets fascinate us even though we know that they are only fiction. How much stronger, then, must be the appeal of true accounts of such achievements. In these stories there is tremendous appeal for both old and young who are looking for romance and adventure and for an insight into the tough and fascinating life of the Old Days in the Golden West.

THE AUTHOR.

JOHN D. MITCHELL,
Chandler, Arizona.
August, 1933.

"STRANGER Tales than these
are told—
But none so True,
so exact, so bold."

—Anon.

TRUE TALE OF THE SEVEN CITIES OF CIBOLA

The Seven Cities of Cibola, said to have been found by followers of Cortez, were located in a valley six leagues long. They have been the object of search by three generations of men and have ever proved a will-of-the-wisp to lure prospectors and adventurers and even military expeditions.

In the year 1528, Cabeza de Vaca and Black Stephen the Moor, then a boy about 17 years of age, were shipwrecked on the coast of Florida. After wandering for eight years they were found by a party of Spaniards scouting near the Gulf of California. Upon arrival at the City of Mexico, Cabeza de Vaca told of having seen much and heard more. Among other things were the Seven Cities of Cibola, located in an unknown land somewhere to the northwest.

The Viceroy Mendoza sent Fray Marcos de Niza to explore the country and if possible find the Seven Cities that were said to contain gold without end. Ahead of Fray Marcos went Black Stephen the Moor, who had been with Cabeza de Vaca. When four days out from San Miguel de Culiacan, at that time located on the coast of Nueva Viscaya, later in the Interdencia de Sonora, and included in what is now the State of Sinaloa, Stephen sent word that he had seen the Seven Cities of Cibola, and they contained more riches than the palaces of Montezuma.

Fray Marcos de Niza relayed the message to Viceroy Mendoza at Mexico City. Shortly after sending the report Black Stephen was captured by the Indians, but was not killed, as is generally supposed.

Fray Marcos de Niza, believing that Stephen had been killed, continued on alone in search of the seven cities. Misled by the Indians, he was taken five or six hundred miles to the north into New Mexico, where he was shown one of the seven little Indian villages located on the headwaters of three different rivers, but which could not possibly be the Seven Cities of Cibola, as they were located in a "continuous" valley six leagues long.

Fray Marcos de Niza returned to the City of Mexico and reported to Mendoza that he had seen one of the wonderful cities and that the others were no doubt fully as rich as reported. So in the year 1540 Don Francisco Vasquez de Coronado, arrayed in his golden armor and mounted on a prancing steed, rode out from Culiacan at the head of 300 Spaniards and 800 Indians under orders from the Viceroy to search out the Seven Cities of Cibola for the Crown of Spain. With Coronado and his glittering column went Fray Marcos de Niza. They followed the same route that Fray Marcos de Niza had taken before, passing down the San Pedro and crossing the mountains into New Mexico, where they reached the poor little Indian villages. Disgusted and disappointed at finding no gold, they finally returned to Mexico.

Black Stephen the Moor, the one man that had really looked upon the seven golden cities, was now a prisoner. Having no means of communicating with Fray Marcos de Niza or Coronado, Black Stephen kept a record of his experiences with the Indians. According to this record the Seven Cities of Cibola were located in a "continuous" valley six leagues long near the Mesa del Toro. The cities, or large community houses all painted white and surrounded by green foliage, presented a beautiful sight when looked upon from surrounding hills.

Being miners themselves and living in a rich mineral region, the Aztecs possessed a large amount of gold, silver and turquoise. In the year 1530 Cortez sent soldiers from Tecovallo to take possession of the west coast. The Spanish soldiers were unable to dislodge the Indians until 1611. In the meantime the riches from the seven cities was collected and stored in a cave before the great battle was fought. The Indians abandoned the cities and concentrated on the Mesa del Toro, or Flat Top Mountain, where the great battle was fought.

The Indians were defeated and forced back to Tubares. In this fight the Indians lost their King. Black Stephen the Moor, then 97 years of age and too old to travel, was killed by the Indians. During the time that he had been held in captivity, Black Stephen had been given a wife who bore him four children. It was from this woman that General Antonio Gomez obtained the record kept by Black Stephen, and which is now owned by the family of Don Inocente Cinfuentes, of Choix, Sinaloa.

After being stripped of their riches, which amounted to several tons of gold and silver vessels and ornaments, the cities were abandoned and fell into decay. Some of the walls of the old buildings can still be seen with large mesquite trees growing through them and covered with morning glory vines.

Those who would search for the Seven Cities of Cibola and the great riches that they contained should remember that they were located in a valley six leagues long, according to the record left by Black Stephen the Moor.

ON "MESA OF THE BULLS" OLD MOCHOMO KEEPS ANCIENT INDIAN SECRET

Up in the foothills of the Sierra Madre on the eastern border of the State of Sinaloa, Mexico, lies the Mesa del Toro, the scene of the last great struggle between the Spanish and the Indians for the possession of the west coast of Mexico.

In the year 1530 Cortez sent a detachment of soldiers from the City of Tecovallo to explore the west coast. In 1531, Nuno de Guzman, President of the Audencia, founded Culiacan, while searching for the fabled land of the Amazons. Guzman heard vague rumors of the Seven Cities a few leagues to the north, but never reached them, because of ill-health and a depleted army. The story of the Seven Cities received no attention due to the inquisition of Guzman, he having revolted against Cortez and the King.

Francisco de Ibarra was the next man to attempt the subjugation of this territory in 1563, but did not succeed in conquering the Mayo and Tarahumarris Indians in the vicinity of Choix, Sinoloa. About thirteen years later, or in 1576 and 1577, a plague broke out among the Mayo and Tarahumarris Indians and it was estimated that about 2,000,000 of their number had perished. This gave the soldiers of Moya y Contreras under Pedro Sanches the advantage and in the spring of 1583 they had driven the Indians under Troano (whose code of laws exist among the Indians at the present time) up to the mountains. Here the Indians made their final stand and succeeded in standing the Spaniards off until May, 1611.

The Indians had fortified the Mesa del Toro, a natural stronghold about 30 miles from Choix on the Choix River. Here Moya y Contreras made several attacks on the Indians but was repulsed with heavy loss. Estevan (Cortez' negro Mozo who introduced the smallpox into Mexico) was taken prisoner in 1539 while scouting ahead of Marcos de Niza, and as he had no other means of communicating with his former captain, he wrote on tepolcates a record or history of the Indians and the record is still in existence. According to these records, in the spring of 1539 Estavan was taken prisoner and the Indians amputated both of his legs to keep him from escaping. They also gave him a wife to cheer his lonely condition and it was from this woman that Estevan obtained most of his knowledge of the Indians and their life. As the Indians had lost a large number of their warriors by the plague and in the war the king of the tribe was obliged to put every available man into action to hold his position, and he called in conference the heads of all the warriors and told them to bring all their treasure before the king. This amounted to several tons of gold and silver ornaments. Before this it had taken a small army to look after the treasure. The king ordered all valuables placed in the "Cuavo pinto" or

The Superstition Mountains

painted cave, which, according to the records, is located on the west bank of the Arroyo del Toro.

The king gave the following orders: "I will stand with my back to the toro (a large rock, resembling a bull) on the 22nd of June, 1609, and where the shadow strikes on the opposite bank of the arroyo in the morning, all valuables must be placed in a cave built for the purpose and a guard placed over the cave night and day." This according to the records was done, giving the tribe an additional several hundred men.

Viceroy Velasco appointed Fontanis, one of the Jesuit Priests from Durango as head of an expedition to dislodge the Indians in 1610. In the same year the Spanish founded Fuerte, Choix and the little town of Torro, about 15 miles from Choix. General Antonio Gomez, under orders from Fontanis, established strongholds at Toro, and Choix, and in the same year treated with the Indians, but not until Gomez had driven them from their stronghold on the Mesa del Toro back to Tobares, and in the fight killed their King.

Estevan was killed by the Indians as he was unable to travel. He left four children, two by his wife and two by a mistress. And it was from the mothers of these children that General Gomez obtained the records left by Estevan.

In the fight the Indians were so completely routed they had to leave their treasure behind, the main part of which has never been recovered. However, placer miners occasionally wash out of the Arroyo del Toro, breast pins, earrings, and finger rings and many other ornaments of gold and silver of odd and quaint design. Most of the ornaments are washed out by an old Indian called "Mochomo" or large black ant, who wanders around that part of the country and many believe that the job of watching the great treasure has been handed down to him. There can be no information extracted from him, not even by his fellow tribesmen, who have become more civilized.

Many thousands of tomahawks and arrow-heads are strewn over the Mesa del Toro and many rock crosses mark the final resting places of the Spanish and the ancient braves that passed on to the happy hunting grounds.

MONTEZUMA'S CASTLE

TREASURE AT BACHACA

In 1767 a delegation of Mayo Indians arrived at
Alamos and persuaded Padre Almada to go with them
to see a rich silver vein that had been discovered
about seven leagues to the southwest at a place called
Bachaca, which is the Indian name for waterfalls.

The mine proved to be of great richness, and the
padre was so pleased with the mine and the beautiful
place in which it was located that he at once decided
to establish an outpost of the church there. The foundations of a chapel and other large buildings were
laid, and the Indians were eager to do the work. The
buildings were made of white tufa stone, an abound-
ance of which is found in the immediate vicinity.
When the chapel was completed it was made a visita
of the church at Alamos.

Water from the hills tumble down through two arroyos into the little valley where they unite and pass
through a narrow gorge over a shelf of rock and into
a shady pool 100 feet below. A dam was constructed
across this narrow outlet, and the water behind it
formed a beautiful lake on the valley floor. The over-
flow from the lake continued to go over the falls and
herds of deer came down from the hills to drink from
the shady pool that it formed beneath the trees. Large
beautifully colored parrots built their nests in the
cliffs high above the falls and flocks of parrakeets

were continually flying back and forth between their
feeding grounds and roosting place near the lake.

The houses for the Indians that worked the mine
were built on the west side of the valley near the
high canyon wall. When the moon shed its silvery
lights over the valley the strains of a guitar would
float across the lake on the warm night air. Suddenly dark clouds would roll across the moon and the
sky blaze with soundless flashes of lightning, without
the faintest rumble of thunder or a drop of rain. Occasionally the stillness of the night was broken by the
distant howl of a wolf or the screeches of an awaken-
ed flock of parrots. High up on the mountain at the
mouth of the mine the Mayo River could be seen in
the distance and the silver crested waves of the Pacific breaking against the shore.

In 1823 a large band of Chihuahua Indians swooped
down through the Chinipas Pass and attacked the
town of Alamos and the surrounding mines. A large
number of the inhabitants were killed, including many
of the Indians at Bachaca.

Many years later a workman, while excavating near
the old house, uncovered a large cement slab with an
iron ring fastened to it. When this slab was lifted,
it disclosed an underground room, in which was found
three large ollas filled with Spanish money, and in
one corner of the room 750 bars of silver bullion.

If you love a flaming sunset, a shining lake in the
noonday sun, the tumbling glory of a waterfall, the
howl of a wolf in the lonely night—you will love old
Bachaca.

TWO SUNS EAST

About 75 miles, or two suns, as an Indian measures distance, east of Ajo, Arizona, on the northern edge of the Santa Rosa country, is a rich gold ledge or chimney running thousands of dollars to the ton. Many of the Indians now living, knew the old Papago that worked the mine. When in need of money with which to buy food the old man would leave the village early in the morning and always return before dark with a small sack full of the rich rock which he gave to his squaw to grind in a metate to free the gold from the rock. The gold would then be sold to merchants in Casa Grande, Ajo or Gila Bend.

Many years passed and the old man made frequent trips to the mine, each time returning with a sack of gold ore. When too old and feeble to travel any more, he told his grandson about the mine and how to find the entrance that was always covered up with a large flat rock. The old man died and passed on to the happy hunting grounds, leaving the grandson in possession of the secret.

A drought came upon the Indian country and food was scarce so the young Indian set out to find the mine. Many trips were made to the mountain where the old man said the gold was located, but no trace of it could be found. The flat rock had become covered with earth. The young Indian came to Ajo and appealed to the writer for assistance to locate the mine. He was accompanied by an old Indian and said the trip could be made on mules in two suns. The route led across the Ajo Valley, covered with mesquite and grease wood, and then up over the old Indian trail to a large tank of clear water near the summit of the first range of mountains. Thousands of quail and doves came to this tank for water.

The mules were hobbled in a patch of luxuriant grass that grew nearby and while the coffee was boiling and the meat roasting on a bed of hot coals, a large coyote attracted by the fresh meat appeared on the top of a small hill a short distance away. I picked up my 30-30 rifle and was in the act of shooting the animal when the old Indian laid his hand on my arm and asked me not to do so. Curious to know the reason why he did not want the animal shot, I asked him to explain. He replied that it might be his grandmother as the Indians believed that after death the spirit of their grandmothers always came back in the form of a coyote. I told him that I had always been under the impression that it was their mother-in-law that came back as a coyote. He looked serious for a moment and replied if that was correct, to go ahead and shoot. Not being quite sure myself and having no desire to shoot either of his relatives, I let the coyote go.

From the tank the trail led up over the summit and down into a beautiful valley covered with tall grasses. In the center of this valley stands a tabletop mountain where thousands of dead Papagoes lie buried in the loose rock around its base.

The old Indian was bothered with the earache and we had to stop every 10 or 12 miles to allow the younger Indian to pour a can of water in the old man's ear. I have never been able to figure out where all the water went to. It all went in and none came out. It sounded just like he was pouring it in a gopher hole.

We reached the village late and passed the rest of the night in a brush house with a bunch of Indians and a number of mongrel dogs sleeping around a small fire built in the center of the room. Two day's search failed to disclose the location of the mine itself, but a large piece of float picked up in the arroyo on the west side of the mountain, weighed 35 pounds and contained, when broken up, $1200 worth of gold. The young Papago insists, and perhaps correctly, that the rich gold ore is located in that small iron-stained mountain just two suns east of the little mining town of Ajo, Arizona.

LOST NIGGER BEN MINE

When Padre Miguel Hidalgo of Dolores, Guanajuato, Mexico, started his revolution in 1810 he performed a great service to his country, but worked a hardship on adventurers and lost mine hunters the world over. Ever since 1820 when the revolution succeeded in freeing 16 million Mexicans and Indians from Spanish rule, miners and adventurers have been flocking into Mexico and all that part of the Southwest that belonged to Mexico at that time, looking for lost mines and buried treasures left by the fleeing Spaniards.

The measurements are all in leagues and varas and the distances are approximate, so if you don't find the stuff where it should be look poco mas alla (a little further on.) It may be in the next county or the next state, but rest assured it is there for they didn't take anything with them.

In 1825 came the great Apache uprising, and for a period of 60 years the long peaceful and prosperous region was harried by rapine and murder. Mines were closed and abandoned, towns were deserted, lapsed into ruin, and in many cases were destroyed by the hostiles; while all the roads and trails were lined with the graves of the victims of Apache hatred and cruelty. As a result of joint operation and co-operation of the American and Mexican military forces, in

1886 the blood-thirsty Geronimo and his band of cruel braves were captured in the Sierra Madres and deported. Then dawned a new era for the Southwest.

One of the most fascinating topics in the west is the traditions of its lost mines and buried treasures. Many of these old stories grow in wealth as time passes but it is the belief of the writer that most of them are based on facts. Many rich mines were covered over and abandoned by the Spanish when forced to leave the country by the revolution and the Apache uprising. Others were found by emigrants and miners who were unable to stop and work them at the time of discovery and were prevented from doing so later on by hostile Indians. Thus as time elapsed they became traditions.

One of the richest mines ever discovered in Arizona was known to the Indians as Little Antelope. This mine is located in Yavapai County and known at the present time as Rich Hill. This mine and the gulches around it have produced 20 millions in placer gold. $780,000 in large nuggets were picked up from the surface on top of Rich Hill. $5,000 and $6,000 in large nuggets were often taken from under one large boulder. One man with $60,000 worth of nuggets loaded on a pack mule on his way to California in the early sixties joined a party of American soldiers in order to make the trip in safety.

Mr. Peeples, an Arizona pioneer, took a fortune from a mine on Rich Hill and afterward established a ranch in Peeples Valley. There was employed on this ranch a colored man by the name of Nigger Ben. An Indian one day told Nigger Ben that there was another hill in that vicinity called Big Antelope and much richer than Rich Hill which was known to the Indians as Little Antelope. Nigger Ben engaged the Indian to take him to this hill and on arrival at Sycamore Springs the Indian told Ben the mine was nearby and advised him to look for it himself. A peculiar trait in Indian nature prevented him from taking Ben to the mine. Ben searched for three days for the gold but was unable to locate it and gave up the search. Some months later he induced the Indian to guide him again, but before departing, advised Mr. Peeples of his intentions and asked him to come to Sycamore Springs at a certain date in case he did not return by that time. Ben feared the Indian would kill him after showing him the gold. When Ben failed to return at the appointed time, Mr. Peeples went to Sycamore Springs and found the negro's dead body. To date no gold has ever been found in that vicinity. Big Antelope like the lost Atlantis is still undiscovered.

LOST NUGGET MINE

Out in the Arizona desert, exact location unknown, but supposed to be about a two days' trip for a burro along the east side of the Colorado River south of Topock, is a streak of yellow clay full of gold nuggets. It has been seen by at least two men and $50,000 or $60,000 in gold nuggets has been taken from it at different times.

One day about 30 years ago a man came in from the desert and boarded a Santa Fe train at Needles, California. On the way east he showed the Santa Fe conductor about $30,000 worth of large gold nuggets, stating that he had found them in a streak of yellow clay on the desert south of Topock. He gave the conductor several of the large nuggets and stated that he would return later to work the mine. Several months passed and then one day the man got off the train at Needles accompanied by a younger man whom he introduced to the conductor as his son. The two men were outfitted for the trip, taking supplies sufficient to last them for about two weeks.

When three weeks had passed and the men had not returned to Needles the conductor notified the authorities and a search was made to the south of Topock but no trace of the missing men could be found and the searchers returned to Needles. The conductor then secured the services of two Indian trailers and in about two months from the time they had disappeared into the desert the Indians came upon the dead bodies of the father and son and nearby the carcasses of the burros. The men and burros had been shot and the cargo of gold nuggets stolen. Many trips have been made into the desert in search of the rich diggings but no one else ever brought back any more of the golden nuggets.

Those who would search for the mine would do well to heed the advice of the old Santa Fe conductor and look for a band of yellow clay out on the desert about two days trip for a Rocky Mountain canary to the south of Topock on the east side of the "Silvery Colorado."

CANYON DE CHELLY

CAUGH OIR

Caugh Oir, or Golden Cup, as the name signifies, is an extinct geyser or crater located on top of Rich Hill, about eight miles east of Congress Junction in Yavapai County, Arizona, at an elevation of 5,200 feet above sea level and 2,000 feet above the surrounding plains.

The famous hill was the scene of a great gold rush in the early sixties. A Mexican discovered the gold in the basin on top of the hill while looking for horses that had strayed from the camp of Captain Pauline Weaver and Major A. H. Peeples who had been attracted to the locality by the reports of Indians who came to La Paz and reported the occurrence of much gold farther east of that place. The party happened to camp at the base of Rich Hill after their Indian guide had deserted them on the desert near Wickenburg.

Shortly after the discovery, $780,000 in gold nuggets had been picked up from the top of the hill. Of this amount, $40,000 was found around the rim of the crater and five or six thousand was often taken from under one large boulder. It is estimated that $20,000,-000 was taken from the basin on top of the hill and the gulches that connect with it. This crater threw out hot water and steam for many thousands of years and it is now believed by many to have been the source of all the gold that was found around it. Of the many arroyos that run down the mountain sides, only those three that connect with the crater have ever produced any gold. These channels are all worn smooth by the hot water and gold-bearing material that was thrown out over a long period of time. That gold is capable of solution, and subsequent precipitation by means of underground waters has been repeatedly demonstrated, and it is now believed that the hot water traveling through subterranean depths leached the gold from the rocks and carried it to the surface in solution where it was precipitated in the metallic form as nuggets.

Caugh Oir is now filled with large granite boulders, iron-stained clay, small pieces of iron and pebbles of silica and identical with the gold-bearing material found in the basin and the gulches below the hill. The crater is supposed to be several thousand feet deep and is believed by many to contain many millions in gold nuggets left there when activity in the crater ceased.

As the search for gold and hidden treasure has ever intrigued mankind, it is to be expected that some day tunnels will be run into the mountain to tap the crater and the Golden Cup once more will be made to pour out the great piles of gleaming gold like those found by the pioneers.

TREASURE OF DON FELIPE

In the quaint old town of Alamos lived a wealthy Spaniard. We will call him Don Felipe. His land stretched over vast space covering Rancho Santa Barbara at the base of Guadalupe Mountain, in the foothills of the Sierra Madre range. The Mayo River rushes down through the narrow gorges past Guadalupe, then makes a great bend around a high point of land that juts out to the north and on which stands the old ranch house like a feudal castle, vividly outlined against the sky. From here the river flows gently through the peaceful Mayo Valley and out to the open sea.

My first view of Santa Barbara was from the top of Guadalupe Mountain. From the early morning until nearly noon the saddle mules toiled up the steep trail that leads to the summit from the valley below. A light rain was falling and the clouds hung low over the rugged mountain slopes. About noon we reached the summit and stood in the warm sunlight far above the clouds. In every direction the mountain peaks stood out above the clouds like beautiful islands in a silvery sea.

The clouds parted and there nestling at our feet was old Santa Barbara, "a fairyland in flowers," covered with roses and buginvilaea, and surrounded by orange groves and green fields of growing grain.

Santa Barbara dates back to the time of the Spanish Conquistadores, and was originally owned by Don Felipe, whose only interest in life was the hoarding of gold and silver for his beautiful and only daughter, Clotilde, whose mother had died at her birth. Many peons were employed in the fields to grow and harvest the grain that was needed to supply the wants of the Indians who worked in the great silver mine on Guadalupe Mountain and in the gold mines at Sobia, just over the mountains to the west.

Two or three times a week large numbers of pack mules loaded with gold and silver bars would come down to Santa Barbara from the mines. The tinkling bells on the lead mules could be heard a long way, and Don Felipe often rode out on his mule to meet them. Upon arrival at Santa Barbara, the mules were always taken inside through a large arched doorway and the precious cargo unloaded. The mules would then be loaded with corn and flour and other supplies needed at the mines.

Twice each year a pack train was sent to the City of Mexico, with one-fifth of all the bullion that had been produced from the mines of Don Felipe. This belonged to the King of Spain, and was known as the royal fifth. The years passed and Don Felipe profited greatly from his agricultural and mining operations. Clotilde, who spent much time at the ranch, grew more beautiful as she developed into young womanhood. Like all Spanish girls, she was a born coquette, and few men could look into her beau-

MISSION DOLORES
SAN FRANCISCO CAL

CANDLESTICKS

MORTAR
and
PESTAL

SPANISH
MISSION PERIOD

MISSION
CROSS

POTTERY

CANDLE STICKS

tiful flashing eyes without falling madly in love with her. Three times each week the band played music soft and low, Clotilde, accompanied by Dona Maria, her duena, strolled among the flowers on the plaza in front of the little white chapel where she often went to pray.

When the revolution broke out in 1810 Santa Barbara was attacked by Indians and Don Felipe was killed by an arrow shot from the bow of a Yaqui warrior. Upon seeing her father fall, Clotilde rushed to his side and was about to be captured, when she suddenly drew from under her mantilla a large picture of the Saint Guadalupe, which she held before her. When the Indians saw their patron saint, they fled in great disorder. Dona Maria took Clotilde to Mexico City and placed her in a convent to be educated. Many years later the search for the mines and great treasure began.

No one knew where Don Felipe hid the bullion after it had been unloaded in the patio. The gold mines at Sobia were relocated and produced a large amount of gold. The Guadalupe Silver Mine has never been found. It was sealed up with all the tools inside. Rumor has it that the treasure was buried in an underground room inside the walls, and that every year a strange light appears in that vicinity.

The Mayo Indians believe that there is something about buried gold and silver that causes it to glow in warm weather when the ground is wet. So every year when the warm June rains begin, they look for the strange lights to appear.

One dark night when a light rain was falling, one of the great spotted jaguars, or Mexican tigers that inhabit the caves on the nearby Moche Cowie Mountains, entered the house of an Indian through an open door and carried off a three-year-old child that was asleep on a pallet near the door. The frantic cries of the mother aroused the village, but the great beast had already carried the child into the thick underbrush, where it could be heard purring and crunching the bones of the little victim.

Just as the Mayos were running to notify the padre at the church, the strange light appeared again inside the walls. All the buildings could be plainly seen in the weird, white, shimmering light.

Every year in June when the rains come, the light appears and the search for the great treasure goes on. The tigers, having tasted man's flesh, come down from the mountain in search of human prey.

LOST BREYFOGLE MINE

In the spring of 1863 a prospector by the name of Breyfogle and a companion passed the Vegas ranch, now Las Vegas, Nevada, on a prospecting trip in the mountains to the south. Breyfogle returned alone to the ranch several days later in almost a perishing condition from thirst and hunger and a fractured skull, but bringing some specimens of very rich ore.

Breyfogle stated that he and his partner camped at a small spring on the side of a high mountain and one day three Indians came to them and told them of a rich gold mine about three miles away. Breyfogle went with the Indians to get samples of the ore, leaving his companion at the camp. Upon his return an Indian walking behind, felled him with a blow on the head and when he regained consciousness, he had a badly bruised head and a fractured skull. The Indians had left him for dead. Breyfogle returned to his camp and found his partner dead and the camp robbed of provisions. He then returned to the Vegas ranch, making the trip in three days without food. Some of the ore was left with Mrs. Stewart, the owner of the ranch, and it has been seen by many prospectors and described as being a pale yellow carbonate ore full of black silver sulphides, horn silver and rich in gold. Ore samples from the mine may also be seen to this day in the old mining camp of Austin, Nevada, and there are living men who knew John Breyfogle who discovered and lost the mine. Breyfogle was never right in the head after receiving the blow and although he was repeatedly grubstaked by different people to hunt for his lost mine, he was never able to locate a place that even looked like his old camp grounds.

It is now believed that Breyfogle's camp was found years later at a small spring in a canyon in the McCullough Mountains about 14 miles northwest of the little town of Searchlight. Parts of cooking utensils and several pieces of the rich ore, like the sample left at the ranch were found near an old campfire by the spring just below the summit of a high mountain.

Old-timers in that part of the country now believe that the mine was later discovered and worked for a short time by an old Mormon from Salt Lake City. This old man made several trips to the McCullough Mountains and each time returned with several burros loaded with rich ore. When he failed to return from his last trip, searching parties found the old Mormon and all his burros shot to death on the bed of a dry lake on the west side of the McCullough Mountains. The old man was very tall with white hair and long white whiskers and searchers sometimes call the Breyfogle the Lost Mormon mine.

LOST SOPORI MINE

On the road from Tucson to the old Spanish town of Arivaca in Southern Pima County, Arizona, stands the shrine of Santa Rita on top of a high promontory just north of the Sopori ranch house and over-looking Sopori Creek and the little cluster of old adobe buildings that stand in the shade of the large cottonwood trees that line the southern bank of the creek.

In the days of the Spanish Conquistadores the Sopori gold and silver mine formed a part of the 21,000 acre ranch. The ore was exceedingly rich in gold and silver and the mine had an extensive reputation in all the territory that formed a part of Mexico at that time. A number of old arrastres in which the rich ore was worked can still be seen in the vicinity. The little Spanish settlement was frequently raided by the Apache Indians and many of the inhabitants killed. There is a tradition that just before one of these raids took place a large amount of gold and silver was buried in one corner of an old adobe house and that it has never been recovered.

The last raid took place long after the American occupation. Several white people were killed and their bodies thrown from the high promontory to which they had fled for safety. One pioneer American woman gave birth to a girl baby while she was being tortured by the Indians. The baby lived and grew to womanhood in Tucson.

The ranch is now owned by a relative of General Robert E. Lee, of Southern fame. Mrs. Lee, the present owner of the ranch, built the little shrine on the high rock several years ago. Travelers passing that way often see women and children kneeling in prayer at the feet of their patron saint, or placing gifts of flowers in the little shrine.

Tradition has it that the work was so badly carried on at the mine that the vein of rich ore was lost. The old rock houses at the mine have long since fallen into decay. The treasure still lies buried in the corner of the old adobe house beneath the cottonwood trees. A few graves nearby tell a story of hardship and suffering endured by the sturdy pioneers that paved the way to civilization in the Great Southwest.

CANYON LAKE

THE LOST TAYOPE MINE

No other mine on the American continent was ever richer, more completely lost or searched for than the lost Tayope Mine.

Mining men from all over the world have searched the mountains of Mexico for this fabulously rich mine supposed to be located in the Sahuaripa district or somewhere near the Vacatete (Cowteat) Mountains in the wild Yaqui Indian country in the State of Sonora, Mexico.

Like most lost mines located in wild Indian country, the Tayope was very rich. The wilder the Indians, the richer the mines seem to be. Old records indicate that several hundred mines were operated in that part of the country during the Spanish occupation and Tayope was the richest of them all.

The mine was supposed to have been discovered about 1635 as records at the old church at Bavispe show that children were brought there from Tayope to be baptised. A church was later built at Tayope and the trips ceased.

In 1767 the Jesuits were expelled from Spain and its possessions and Tayope was sealed up and abandoned. The camp and church was soon thereafter destroyed by Indians. Tradition has it that many millions in gold bullion was sealed up in the mine before it was abandoned by the padres. Many expeditions from Spain and most of the large mining companies in the United States have in years past diligently searched for the wonderful mine.

Some years ago the Mexican government rounded up a large number of Yaqui Indians and deported them to Yucatan. One of these Indians making his way back to his old home in the Vacatete country stopped at the home of the writer, which at that time was in Southern Sonora, Mexico, and asked for food. This Yaqui spoke Spanish, having been employed on a ranch in the Yaqui Valley. Upon being asked if he knew anything about the Tayope mine in his country he replied that it was located some distance to the north of his home in Cerro Azul (Blue Mountain.)

He said the mine was an Antigua and that it had been worked by the Spanish. He further stated that there was the ruins of an old camp and a canal eleven or twelve kilometers long that had been used to bring water to the arrastres in which the gold ore was treated. This canal ended near the ruins of a large church. Five bells of different size were still to be seen near the church.

The Yaqui Indians often hunt deer in that vicinity and have no doubt killed many prospectors that have disappeared while looking for the lost Tayope and the millions in gold bullion stored away in the old mine down in the Vacatete (Cowteat) Mountains of Old Mexico.

LLUVIA DE ORO AND GLORIA PAN MINES

The Lluvia de Oro and the Gloria Pan were two of the richest mines ever discovered in Mexico; the Lluvia de Oro in recent times and the Gloria Pan in the days of the padres.

About 40 years ago a Sinaloa Indian rode out from his mountain home for a little pasear that took him down to a nearby village where the fiesta of San Juan was being celebrated. After having danced the deer and snake dance all night and partaking freely of liquid refreshments he laid down on his serape for a little nap. Soon thereafter another peon happened along that way and overheard him talking in his sleep about two rich mines that he had discovered in the mountains near his home. This peon hurried home and told his patron what he had overheard. Several days later the Indian was induced to show one of his mines which shortly thereafter proved to be one of the richest gold mines ever discovered in Mexico, and on account of the great abundance of free gold in the rock, it was called the Lluvia de Oro (shower of gold.)

In return for showing this great mine the poor Indian was given the meat of an old bull; the patron keeping the hide. Disappointed at the treatment he had received the Indian refused to show the Gloria

Pan to anyone and died some years later taking the secret with him to his grave. The Gloria Pan was discovered in 1750 and was being operated by the Jesuits in 1767 when the Spanish king, Charles III issued the edict that all Jesuits should be expelled from Spain and its possessions. For 17 years the gold from one of the richest mines in Mexico had piled up. There is little doubt that the Jesuits had forseen that they would not be able to take any of their treasure out of the country and that it would possibly be confiscated, for their records brought over from Spain in recent years show that a large number of Indians were employed in carrying the treasure up the mountain and storing it in the mine. When the mine was sealed up it contained several million dollars in gold bars in addition to large bodies of rich gold ore ready to be mined. The Jesuits never were able to take any of their treasure out of the country and left, never to return.

Every year prospectors search the brush-covered hills for the wonderful mine and great treasure, but no trace of it has ever been found. There are other Indians, it is believed, that could reveal the hiding place, but they refuse to guide any one to the Gloria Pan on account of the treatment received by their countryman after showing the Lluvia de Oro.

By his mistreating the poor Indian the old patron lost a chance to add several million dollars to his wealth, but at the same time he established the record for the highest price ever paid for a Mexican bull hide.

LOST ESCALANTE MINE

The lost Escalante Mine and its great store of gold bars is one of the celebrated traditions of the west. Much time and money has been spent in the quest for this fabulously rich mine supposed to be located somewhere in the Santa Catalina Mountains just north of Tucson, Arizona.

The Escalante is also called the Mine with the Iron Door. Padre Escalante who first worked the mine was an assistant to Padre Kino at the Mission San Xavier del Bac. The main work of Padre Escalante was mines and mining. He traveled all over Pimeria Alta to investigate the mines and to collect the church's share of the gold and silver. The records left, if any, by Escalante should be helpful in tracing down those old mines.

Calistro, the old Opata Indian, living down on the Santa Cruz River near the ancient ruins of the Tumacacori Mission, had been telling me stories about the many old mines worked by the Jesuit priests during the Spanish occupation. An Indian so well posted, I thought, should be able to tell me something about the famous Escalante Mine worked by the Spanish in the sixteenth century. I was not mistaken.

"My grandfather," said Calistro, "was a very old man when I was just a small boy. He knew many stories about rich mines found and worked by the Spaniards. I used to make many trips along the river and into the mountains with him hunting for woodrats with which to make soup. One evening after we had caught about two dozen rats and sat down to rest on a large rock near a pool of water that stood in the bed of the Canada del Oro, he pointed up to the Santa Catalina Mountain and said the Escalante gold mine is located in that mountain and that it was one of the richest gold mines that had ever been discovered in Pimeria Alta (as this part of the country was called at that time.)''

This wonderful mine was discovered by Indians while hunting deer in the Santa Catalinas in 1698 and was worked for many years by Father Escalante, a Jesuit priest. This wonderful mine was located on the western slopes of the mountains and not far from the Ventana (a hole in the rocks resembling a window.) On a clear day the miners, when standing at the mouth of the tunnel, could see the light shining through the Ventana near the summit of the mountain in a southeasterly direction from where they stood.

Much free gold was picked up from the surface of the ground where the wonderful vein outcropped, and the heavy rains that had for centuries fallen in the Santa Catalinas had washed the loose gold down the mountain sides into the Canada del Oro and made the great placer deposits located there.

Many Indians were employed at the mine, getting out the gold ore which was then packed down to the foot of the mountain where it was ground in arrastres and then smelted into gold bars and stored away in a strong room built for the purpose.

For many years the work went on and the mine grew richer as the tunnel penetrated farther into the mountain. Then one day when the miners were all away at a fiesta, a large band of hostile Indians swooped down on the camp and after killing all the women and children and the old men that had remained in the camp that morning, the entrance to the mine was destroyed and covered over. The place was deserted on account of the great Indian uprising and to this day the wonderful mine on the mountainside and the strong room full of gold bars down the trail that leads to the Canada del Oro (Grand Canyon) remains unseen. Calistro, the last of the Opatas, now sleeps by the side of his grandfather down on the banks of the Santa Cruz.

LOST SOAPMAKER MINE

All lost mines are supposed to be fabulously rich. The longer they are lost the richer they seem to get. The lost Soapmaker mine is no exception to this rule.

In the year 1850 a small party of Mexicans on their way to California from the little town of Caborca, in the State of Sonora, Mexico, passed through what is now the southwest part of Pima County, Arizona. They were making for a crossing on the Colorado River near the present town of Yuma, where they hoped to strike a trail that was afterward known as the Butterfield stage route.

They camped one night near Tinaja Alta, about 70 or 80 miles west of the present mining town of Ajo. Some of the pack animals strayed off during the night and the next morning while out looking for them a Mexican climbed up the side of a small round mountain in order to get a better view of the surrounding country and if possible locate the missing animals. He had only gone a short distance when his attention was attracted to a very rich vein of gold ore protruding through the sand that was piled up on the south side of the mountain. Further investigation revealed a vein about two feet wide very rich in gold. There was a streak of strawberry colored quartz about seven or eight inches wide running along the

hanging wall side of the vein that was matted together with wire and coarse gold.

Before returning to camp with the animals the Mexican noted the surroundings to make sure that he
could return again and find the vein. He noted that
the vein was slowly being covered over by drifting
sand that the south winds daily blew up from the
desert below. To the west from where he stood he
could see Cabesa Prieto (Black Head) Mountain outlined against the sky. The mountain was small and
round and the vein about one-third of the way up the
south side was running in a northwesterly and southeasterly direction. After taking a few samples of the
ore he returned to camp and shortly thereafter left
the party, returning to Caborca in order to get help
to work the mine. A German soapmaker at Caborca
was interested in the venture and was soon on his
way to the mine with two Mexicans and a pack outfit
loaded with provisions and tools sufficient to work
the mine. Upon reaching the country where the mine
was located they camped at a small spring some distance to the south and there built an arrastre to grind
the ore in. They made several trips to the mine and
each time returned with the pack animals loaded
down with the rich ore. Then one day when they
were all at the mine taking out ore, three young Papago Indians appeared at the top of the shallow shaft
and shot them full of arrows before they could escape. Making sure that they were all dead, the Indians then filled the hole with cactus and sand and

after robbing the camp left the vicinity, never to return.

Relatives of the murdered men from Caborca made several trips to the vicinity but were never able to locate the mine or get any trace of the three men. When old "Doctor" Juan, a Papago Indian, dictated this way-bill he was on his death bed and was the sole survivor of the little band of Indians that had killed the miners 70 years before and kept the secret from Mexicans and white men alike.

Very rich float has in years past been picked up by prospectors and cowmen in that vicinity and hardly a year passes that some expedition outfitted from Yuma or Ajo does not head into the desert wastes in search of this wonderful mine. A million dollars in gold could quickly be taken from such a vein as the one described by "Doctor" Juan. The Papagos say that sometime when the moon is right the windmaker will send down a cold north wind to blow the sand away again, uncovering the wonderful vein.

Paradise of the Treasure Hunter

THE MINES OF LATOUCHE

The great copper deposits on Latouche Island in Southwestern Alaska were worked by the Indians long before the Russians or Americans came to Alaska. The Aleut Indians made their homes on Latouche and that they chose a beautiful place in which to live cannot be disputed. They made their living by hunting and fishing. During the salmon run each year large numbers of the fish would be dried and smoked and stored away for food during the long cold winter months when the snow was too deep for them to venture out in search of food.

The bright colored copper ore was mined with stone hammers and ground into a powder from which they made a paint for their sealskin boats. These large beautifully colored boats were envied by all the other tribes. The fierce Yakutat Indians inhabited the region around Yakutat Bay not far from Malaspini and Muir Glaciers. The Yakutat were a strong warlike tribe and often made war on the Aleuts. In these battles the Yakutat would take many prisoners and then exchange them for copper ore which they used to paint their own boats.

About the first of April every year, the warm Japanese current strikes the Alaskan coast and the snow and ice melt rapidly and beautiful wild flowers spring up all over the lowlands and many kind of berries ripen during the short summer months. The warm waters caused great icebergs to break from the glaciers and float among the green islands on their way out to the open sea.

One bright spring morning just as the sun rose over the ragged peaks of Knight's Island, one of these beautiful icebergs came floating past Montague Island and was just rounding the point of Latouche, when Okalina, a beautiful maiden of 16 years and daughter of the Aleut Chief, started out in her little sealskin canoe for a trip along the north side of the island to pick blue berries that grew in profusion on some parts of the island. There was something fascinating in the wild solitude of the place that morning and seeing the beautiful iceberg sparkling in the warm sunlight with white sea gulls flying around it, Okalina changed her course and rowed toward it. The great berg vividly outlined against the background of green foliage, looked like a great sailing ship on her way to the sea.

Concealed on the opposite side of the berg was a large number of Yakutat war canoes on their way to Latouche to fight for copper ore. The canoes were in fan shape formation like wild ducks and geese fly. They presented a beautiful appearance as the sun shone on the wet paddles as they were changed from one side to the other. The Indians row by taking two strokes on one side and then all changing at the same time to the other side. When abreast of Latouche, the canoes began to drop from behind the berg and in plain sight of Okalina who was now only a short dis-

tance away. Upon seeing the beautiful girl in her
bright colored boat, the young chief of the Yakutats
was struck with awe and admiration and decided to
capture her at any cost. The warriors still rowing in
fan shape began to spread out from behind and soon
formed a circle around the little boat occupied by
Okalina. The girl stood up in the boat, throwing off
her camalinka, (a garment made from the intestines
of a seal), and for a brief second stood naked before
the young chief and the startled warriors, then she
dove head first into the water and presently appeared
swimming like a sea otter near the surface of the water outside the ring of boats. The young chief sped
forward in his war canoe which was paddled by two
husky warriors and when Okalina came up for air,
he pulled her into the boat.

The Aleuts had been watching the chase from their
village and were now rushing down toward the beach,
whooping and yelling and jumping from side to side
as they prepared to give battle to their enemies that
had now landed and were still holding the struggling
Okalina. The Yakutat chief offered to trade Okalina
for a good supply of copper ore and after much talk,
the deal was made but the girl had fallen in love with
the stalwart young chief and refused to go back to
her own people. The old Aleut chief, anxious to form
an alliance with the Yakutats, agreed to the marriage
and instead of the usual battle, they had a big feast
and after the wedding the Yakutat boats, loaded with
copper ore, glided out into the moonlight on their
way back to their own village.

The years passed and the Yakutats made many trips to Latouche, taking Okalina to visit her people and each time returning with a good supply of copper ore, and their boats, like those of the Aleuts, were the most beautiful in all the country.

The Russians came and then the Americans and the great mine was sold by the Aleuts for $50 and a phonograph. Big Elia and Okalina died and were both buried on Latouche. Now when the warm Japanese current strikes the Alaskan shore, wild flowers spring up around their graves and great butterflies float overhead in the warm sunlight. When the moon hangs low over the island, the fierce Malamute and huskies point their noses high in the air and howl like the gray wolves that roam over the tundras in search of food. The Aleuts say that the spirit of Okalina comes back every year to the beautiful island of Latouche in the far-off Pacific.

LOST SIX-SHOOTER MINE

One who has never seen a sandstorm on the desert has failed to see nature in her ugliest mood. The sun hangs like a golden disc in the darkened sky and the wind swirls over the desert, whipping the sand dunes into fantastic shapes and the small particles of sand, driven by the force of the wind, cut like points of steel. The sun disappears behind the dark clouds of sand and dust, and darkness falls over the face of the desert. The wind sweeps the ground clean in one spot only to pile the sand high in another.

It was into such a storm as this that the superintendent of the Planet Mine, in Yuma County, Arizona, rode about 50 years ago, while on his way back to the mine after having accompanied a party of investors from the mine to the nearest stage station at Quartsite. Horse and rider became lost in the storm which lasted for several days and after wandering in circles and zig-zagging until tired out the man sat down on a ledge of rock that outcropped in the sand. The rock stood up several feet above the desert floor and offered some protection against the storm. Crouching down beside it, he placed his coat over his head and shoulders and in that way kept out the drifting sand.

When the storm finally passed over and the desert became calm again, he noticed that the ledge that had protected him from the storm was quartz and that it was full of free gold. He managed to break off a few pieces of the ore which he put into his pockets and then took a note book from his pocket and made a note of the location, describing it the best he could. He then took off his two 45 six-shooters and placed them beside his coat on top of the ledge of wonderful ore in order that he might return and claim the mine.

The miner and horse were both weak from having wandered for several days and nights on the desert without food or drink and could scarcely walk. The desert landmarks were now clearly outlined against the sky and the man headed the weakened horse in the direction of the Planet Mine and he held to the tail of the horse for support. How far he traveled in this way is not known but the horse came into camp and was found standing at the corral gate.

Searching parties found the dead body of the superintendent near the edge of the desert where he had fallen when too weak to hold on to the horse's tail any longer. In his pockets were found several pieces of the rich ore and the note describing the location. The ore assayed $25,000 per ton.

Prospectors and desert rats claim that what the sandstorms cover up one time, they may uncover the next. Although more than 50 years have passed and men have scoured the desert in every direction, no trace of the lost Six-Shooter Mine has ever been found.

THE GLORY HOLE

In the summer of 1909 three Arizona prospectors, Alger, Barker and Griffin, were prospecting for gold in the Harquavar Mountains about 12 miles northwest of Salome in Northern Yuma County, Arizona. Alger had picked up a very rich piece of gold ore in that vicinity about twenty years before and had been coming back every year thereafter to look for the vein. Provisions were running short and the three partners had about given up hopes, when Alger discovered the wonderful cropping of gold ore from which the rich specimen that he had picked up 20 years before had come.

Three sacks of the ore were taken to Phoenix and displayed. The ore assayed $338,510.00 per ton.

When the news of this find was published throughout the United States, a stampede was in process, and what promised for a time to be one of the greatest gold rushes known to mining history, was under way. Prospectors and capitalists from all over the United States rushed into the new camp and ground was located for many miles in every direction from the new find.

Salome and Vicksburg were both booming and a new town called Winchester had sprung up at the

Old Desert Mine about three miles south of the Glory Hole.

One look at the wonderful ore was enough to start the newcomers off into the hills to locate claims on which they hoped to find more of the yellow metal so abundantly exposed at the Glory Hole.

After locating their claims, the stampeders spent most of their time killing rattle snakes and Gila monsters.

One day shortly after the boom started, the sheriff and a number of deputies swooped down on the camp and picked up Henry Starr, the noted Oklahoma bandit that had been attracted to the camp by the reports of the rich gold ore to be found there.

Several small deals were put through and just at a time when a great array of capital was in process of being lined up to operate some of the other mines, the Glory Hole pinched out and the boom that was just getting into full swing pinched out with it and the camp was soon deserted.

Considerable work was done on the Glory Hole property some years later but no more of the wonderful ore was ever found there. A large amount of high grade ore was taken from the original find by the parties that leased it from the discoverers.

THE GOLDEN BEANS

In the Sixteenth Century when the Spanish were operating many gold and silver mines in Mexico, the Old Padre in the little town of Camoa on the Mayo River in Southern Sonora, could stand at the door of his church and look in a southeasterly direction directly into the mouth of a tunnel on the side of a large mountain that rises from the plain like an immense black balloon. It was known to the Mayo Indians as Oro Muni (Gold Beans), so-called on account of the large number of gold nuggets resembling beans that were found in the arroyos running down from the mountain. The padre sent out miners and discovered the ledge from which the gold had eroded. A large amount of gold was taken from the vein and the mountain side and smelted into bullion. The miners could, on a clear day, look down from the mountain and see the church and hear the bells ring.

When the Jesuits were expelled from Mexico, the mine was sealed up, with all the bullion that had been taken from it, stored away in the back end of the tunnel. The town was destroyed and the inhabitants moved away. The location was lost for 200 years or more and then a new town sprung up not far away and the search for the mine began. The ruins of the old church were excavated and a large solid gold crown and a heavy gold dagger belonging to the Saint Nuestra Senora de Las Dolores, were found and may now be seen in the new church at Camoa. Mexican and Indian Vaqueros, riding after cattle on the mountain and through the wilderness of cactus and bush-covered land around it, claim to have seen the old dumps below the tunnel, but no amount of money would induce them to show the location.

In the rainy season dark clouds hang over the mountain and sheets of still, tropical lightning run up and down the ridges. Torrents of water rush down the sides, washing the golden beans into the arroyos below. Strange lights are seen by the natives around the old church and many holes have been dug by searchers looking for the Padre's gold.

One dark night not many years ago, a strange light appeared near the old church, and the Indians were afraid to go near it although they said that wherever one of these strange lights appeared, gold was sure to be found. An old Indian, that was considered a Big Hombre in the tribe, vounteered to drive a stake where the light appeared so the treasure could be dug up on the following day. A short stake was procured and when the Indian bent over to drive it into the ground, he drove it through the corner of his blanket. When he started to leave, he felt a tug at his blanket and thought that the dead patron, that the Spanish always left to guard their treasure, had captured him. The poor fellow fainted and had to be rescued by the other Indians. No more digging has been done in that vicinity since. The mine up on the mountainside, with its great pile of gold and silver bars, is still undiscovered.

THE QUINTERA MINE

The Quintera was one of the famous silver mines of Mexico, having first been discovered and worked by the Spanish until they were driven from Mexico in 1823. Without doubt mining was the principal industry during the period of Spanish occupation through three centuries of time and some of the richest in the world were discovered and worked during that time. The Quintera was first worked by the Spanish that founded the old town of Guadalupe on the banks of the Mayo River about 20 miles west of the mine in the Almos district of southern Sonora, Mexico.

Ore from the Quintera and other rich mines on the same vein was packed down to Guadalupe and there worked out, the old ruins of which can still be seen near the old tumbled down church and about 100,000 tons of slag piled up near the banks of the Mayo River.

After the Spanish had been driven from Mexico in 1823 the mine fell into the hands of the Almada family of Alamos and a new town and smelter was built near the Quintera. This town was called Aduana and located in a narrow canyon below a high mountain peak called La Cacharamba. This wonderful mine has produced over 100,000,000 pesos in recent times and was in operation until about 20 years ago. It is owned at the present time by the Bank of Egypt, of Paris, France.

The early operation of the mine after the Spanish were driven from Mexico laid the foundation for the fortune of the Almadas. The founder of the family to make fittingly the wedding of his daughter the first bride of the Almadas, lined the bridal chamber in his beautiful mansion with bars of silver and paved with bars of silver the walk trodden by the bridal party across the plaza from the door of the Almada mansion to the door of the church; and treading upon these uncounted riches, the bridal party marched to the altar.

Besides the millions that this wonderful mine has produced in recent times, several expeditions have been sent over from Spain to search for other millions, which according to tradition, were left buried in or near the old church in the ancient town of Guadalupe.

BLACK GOLD

Away off to the northeast of Indio, California, and 60 miles from the nearest water hole, there is a land of mystery and adventure unequalled in all the Great Southwest.

Strange stories come out of this land of heat-torn and blackened rocks. Strange things have happened in this no-man's land; grinning skulls stare from the burning sands and piles of bleaching bones mark the dim trails that lead out into the last of the bad lands of the Old West.

Indians tell of immense quantities of gold scattered about the floor of what seems to be the remnants of an extinct volcano or a mineralized cone. The gold is tarnished black like the rocks in which it is found. Rain seldom falls in this desolate spot, and no vegetation ever grows there. Not even a jackrabbit or a lizard can survive the awful heat of this desert waste.

Only two men, one of whom was an Indian, ever entered this valley of gold and lived to tell the tale. These men spent five years in establishing stations and caches of water and provisions that finally enabled them to reach the golden crater. On the last lap of the journey they had to dismantle their wagon and let it down over the rimrock into the valley below with a windlass and ropes.

A narrow crevice was found in the wall, and the two mules were led down through this. When within five or six miles of their destination the wagon was left behind and the trip finished on the mules.

The dim trail that they followed to the mine was strewn with the skeletons of Indians that had reached the mine and died on the way out. A small pile of black gold was found by each skeleton, and empty ollas or water bottles, indicating that they had perished from thirst and heat. Ten or twelve dead Indians were found along this one dim trail, and there were, no doubt, many others on other trails leading into the desert. About $10,000 in gold was picked up near the skeletons, and upon reaching the crater they found the floor of it literally covered with nuggets and slabs of black gold. Thousands— millions of dollars worth of gold was scattered about among the rocks and sticking out of the volcanic ashes.

The two men remarked that a railroad engine could not haul all the gold that they saw scattered over the ground at their feet. They managed to reach the wagon with $65,000 worth of the gold. Upon their return from the crater they were more dead than alive, and were never able to make a second trip to the valley of gold.

The white man purchased an orange grove near Redlands, California, and just before his death told two friends the location of the wonderful deposit of black gold.

GOOD MEDICINE AND BURIED GOLD AT AJO

There is a tradition among the Papago Indians that in by-gone days long before the Americans came to this part of the country the arroyos around the great copper mines at Ajo were worked by the Papago Indians for placer gold. This seems probable as the great ore bodies at the present time carry about 20 cents per ton in gold. The erosion for untold centuries carried this gold down from the hillsides and concentrated it as placer on the bottom of the arroyos,

The Papagoes established their village near the mines and made their living by panning gold and killing the wild game that roamed over the boundless plains below the mines. The country at that time belonged to Mexico, so every year the Papago chief led his people down to Caborca, in the Altar district, to barter their gold for supplies.

The Mexicans discovered the source of the gold and sent an expedition of about 500 men to Ajo to work the mines. The Mexicans brought provisions and supplies sufficient to enable them to work the mines for a year before returning to Caborca to market their gold. Upon arrival at the mines the Indians were forced to abandon the workings. Being a gentle people toward the Mexicans, they left the mines without a fight.

The Mexicans established their camp in the vicinity and took out a large amount of gold. After they had worked the placers for six or eight months, a large band of Apache Indians on their way from the gulf to their stronghold in the Superstition Mountains to gather fruit from the Saguaro Cactus that grows profusely in the foothills of the Superstitions, swooped down upon them from the nearby mountains. The surprised Mexicans put up a stiff fight but being outnumbered and practically without arms of any kind at the time, they were finally defeated and forced to flee for their lives. So completely were they routed that they had to abandon their dead and all the supplies including their guns and a large amount of gold buried in the camp. Their first stop was at the Sonoita River, about 35 miles south of the mines, from where they made their way to Caborca, never to return again.

The Papagoes that had been forced by the Mexicans to give up the mines were watching the fight from the surrounding hills. The Apaches had made many raids upon the Papagoes and consequently they were deadly enemies. Seeing that the Mexicans had abandoned the field and fled to Sonoita, the Papagoes now considered it time for them to act. The Apaches were heavily armed, each carrying a long bow and a quiver of arrows and most of them had large tomahawks in their belts. The Papagoes were unarmed. They didn't need any. Their medicine man carried a buckskin sack full of a mysterious powder that he considered strong medicine for just such an occasion.

San Jose de Tumacacori Mission, Founded by Father Kino in 1692 A. D.

By Norman G. Wallace

This powder when thrown into the air would start a whirlwind that would destroy everything in its path. The chief held up his right hand as a signal for silence. Every warrior stopped and remained motionless. The medicine man untied the buckskin sack, took out a large handful of powder, throwing it high into the air just as the warriors let out a blood-curdling war whoop that shook the very hills as it echoed back and forth across the canyons. Almost immediately, as if by magic, a great funnel-shaped whirlwind was seen to drop out of the eastern sky and come rushing into the west, headed straight for the Apache camp. Nearer and nearer came the great whirlwind, tearing up trees by the roots and bending the greasewoods and sage brush to the ground like grass.

The Papago warriors were leaping down the hillsides toward their ancient enemies that could now be seen standing on a long ridge, plainly outlined against the deep blue sky. A large number of squaws and papooses that had accompanied the bucks on the trip to the Gulf were returning to their mountain homes and like the warriors they too were mounted on ponies. Frightened almost to death by the hideous yelling of the Indians and the terrible noise of the whirlwind that was now kicking up large clouds of dust, the ponies stampeded and headed for the tall tulies, bucking the squaws and papooses off as they went. The Apache warriors thunderstruck with fear and superstition, were having a hard time controlling their own horses that were trying frantically to join the others rushing down toward the flats below. The Papago warriors were racing down upon them from the south and west, yelling like demons, and the great whirlwind coming out of the east directly toward them, the Apaches were consternated. Nothing like this had ever happened to them before, so they abandoned the field without a fight and by the time they got the squaws and papooses picked up and back on their ponies again the Papagoes were right behind them, and, to make it even worse, another whirlwind, this time a regular humdinger, was headed across the flats kicking up great clouds of dust and roaring like the devil himself.

After putting their enemies to flight, the Papagoes returned to their old gold diggings where they found enough provisions and supplies to run them for another year. The pot of golden nuggets buried by the Mexicans has never been found.

Now at the same time every year the Papagoes congregate at the village of Moivavi (many wells) for a great fiesta where they celebrate with eating and dancing the victory they won over the Mexicans and Apaches. When the fiesta is over and the stars come out, the medicine man gets out the buckskin pouch from its secret hiding place and ties it up again with a strong string to keep it safe and ready for use in case the Apaches ever come back again.

THE COPPER BOX

Two hundred years before the freedom of the Mexicans and Indians from Spain in 1823, mining operations were carried on by Jesuit and Franciscan priests in the vicinity of the old mining mission of Tumacacori on the Santa Cruz River south of Tucson.

Ore from some of the richest mines in the world was carried on the backs of Indians to the mission where it was melted into bullion. The ruins of the old furnaces can still be seen just east of the mission. Large piles of slag from these operations were discovered by Americans in 1850 and sold at a good profit, as it still contained a large amount of gold and silver.

There is a tradition among the Papago Indians that the mission was attacked about noon one day during the year 1823 by a band of Apache Indians, and a large number of Papagoes killed. The Mexicans and Indians had freed themselves from Spanish rule and Indian raids were becoming more frequent, so the padre decided to abandon the mission and return to Spain.

All the dead killed that day were buried in an underground room near the mission and the entrance was filled with earth. The bullion that had been collected in the mining operations was packed out to the Guadalupe mine, one league southwest of the mission, and placed in the tunnel. The side of the mountain was then blasted down over the opening and all traces of the mine obliterated.

There was 2050 mule loads of silver from the Huachuca and Santa Rita Mountains and 905 loads of gold and silver bullion from the mines of the Tumacacori and Tascosa Mountains. The total value of the gold and silver amounted to about 45 million pesos.

The gold and silver candlesticks and other fixtures from the altar, including a heavy gold crown and jewels belonging to the Saint Guadalupe were placed in a copper box with the church records, maps of the mines and a description of the treasure. This box and other church property was placed on the backs of mules and the trip to the Altar Mission, to the south, was begun.

From Tumacacori the trail led out across the grass covered foothills, then down into a deep canyon to the Guadalupe mine and up through the pines to the summit of the Tumacacori Mountains. The padre stopped on the summit to look at the golden glow of the sunset.

Spreading out below to the east was the beautiful valley of the Santa Cruz and the old white mission standing out like a jewel on the green banks of the river that glistened like a silver thread in the rays of the setting sun as it sank behind the mountains.

After looking for the last time upon the scene, the padre and the little pack train disappeared down the winding trail that led past the Tumacacori mine on the west side of the mountain and one and one-half leagues from the Guadalupe mine. In the vicinity of this mine they met another pack train coming north from the Altar Mission. The padre in charge of this train stated that the Indians had raided his mission and that conditions were also very bad.

The two padres decided to bury their property, including the copper box from Tumacacori, and the Altar fixtures from the Altar Mission, in the Tumacacori mine. This was done and the two padres set out for the coast.

After enduring many hardships they arrived safely in Spain, where they left a record of the mines and treasure. One hundred years later the record was copied and the search for the mines and treasure began.

There is a key to the copper box, and in one corner there is a screw. If the screw is taken out and an iron bar removed, opening the box, the maps of the treasure will be revealed.

THE PADRE'S GOLD AT SONOYTA

The tradition of buried gold at Sonoyta goes back a long ways and for more than 180 years it has been the Eldorado of the Great Southwest. History states that "In 1750 occurred the second revolt of the Pima tribes, in which the missionaries at Caborca and Sonoyta were killed, as were about 100 Spaniards. Bac and Guevavi were plundered and abandoned." History fails to state whether the mission at Sonoyta was ever rebuilt and occupied or not. Only the foundations are now visible.

Tradition among the Papago Indians being more generous furnishes the details. The old Indians say that many years ago a great white ship came sailing over the western sea and anchored in St. George's bay. Many white men came out of the ship and set out across the desert and after traveling a distance of about 80 miles they came to a green spot of surpassing beauty. From the foot of a mountain gushed a crystal stream that flowed for many miles toward the sea before being swallowed up in the sands of the great desert.

The white men made their camp in the shade of the trees that grew along the margin of the beautiful stream. Wild game in countless numbers roamed over the boundless plains and rested in the shade of the trees.

Some of the men hunted wild game and prospected in the nearby mountains while others returned to the ship for supplies. Upon their return from the ship they laid the foundation of a large church. The place was known to the Indians as Sonoyta and had been their camping grounds for years. The padre in charge of the expedition employed Papago and Pima Indians to do the work of building the church and to till the soil. Canals were constructed and water taken from the river to irrigate the crops which consisted of corn, beans, pumpkins, watermelons, cotton and many kinds of fruit such as grapes, peaches, pomegranates grew in profusion near the church.

Placer mines were discovered in the San Francisco Mountains a short distance to the south and when the church was completed a large number of men were put to work in the mines washing out the placer gold which they delivered to the padre. A small furnace was constructed for the purpose of smelting the placer gold and converting it into gold bars. When sufficient gold had been collected it would be run into a bar by the padre and then given to a Mozo (man servant) who would then deposit it in an underground room beneath the mission door.

The mission was finally completed and painted white inside and out. It presented a beautiful appearance when viewed from the surrounding hills. The Indians had never in all their lives seen anything like it. The bells and all the vessels were made of solid gold and silver. Many years passed and the old Mozo made frequent trips to the underground room beneath the mission floor, each time placing a bar of gold on the great pile that gleamed yellow in the dim light of his candle.

As the gold increased the Indians were forced to work harder and longer hours in the mines and the women complained of the hard work in the fields and at the corn grinders which took all their time to feed the hungry miners.

The Indians were a peace-loving people but when oppressed or attacked by an enemy they were as fierce and relentless as the Apaches whom they had often defeated in battle. So while the padre spread the doctrine of Christ and collected gold the Indians secretly talked and planned a revolution that would free them from the white man's religion and oppression. One bright September morning when the sweet toned bells rang out over the upland plains calling the people to early morning prayer, small groups of Indian men could be seen coming across the hills toward the mission. The Indian women did not come to worship that morning. Although it was a warm day, each Indian man was wrapped in a long blanket. When the church was full of warriors the Indian chief and all the head men drew from under their blankets large tomahawks which they immediately sank into the brain of the padre and the two priests that were visiting the mission at that time. The dead bodies of the three priests were thrown into the underground room with the gold and the opening was filled with rock and earth. The roof and walls of the mission were then pulled down. The old Mozo never saw again the great pile of gold bars that gleamed in the faint light of his candle in the dark underground room beneath the mission floor at Sonoyta.

COCOS ISLAND

Many of us are pirates and sea rovers at heart and long to go down to the sea in ships. Pirates and pieces of eight, the Jolly Rover on the Spanish Main, an ancient chart and an old sea chest, a beautiful tropical island in the far off Pacific is the dream of eternal youth. For more than a century this combination has lured adventurers from all over the civilized world to Cocos Island to search for buried treasure. This small island is located about 400 miles west of Columbia and 250 miles north of the equator. It was for many years the hideout of pirates and buccaneers. Wild and blood-curdling are the stories told of happenings there before Captain Graham was sent out by Great Britain to clean it up. Many a sailor walked the plank at Cocos Island, and Graham, so the story goes, was so captivated by the island that he, after chasing the pirates off, turned buccaneer himself.

In addition to many other caches of pirate loot, there is said to be $60,000,000 in gold and silver bullion and precious gems buried somewhere on the island. This treasure belonged to the Peruvian Government and was taken on board a warship for safe keeping when a revolution broke out in 1823. A rebel ship gave chase and in order to keep the treasure from falling into rebel hands it was hurriedly buried on Cocos Island. On the return trip the warship was captured by the rebels and sent to the bottom of the ocean with all hands on board. The question now is what became of the great treasure. Presumably it has never been taken away, and is still buried somewhere on the island.

Many expeditions outfitted at great expense have sailed away to this beautiful little South Sea Island to search for the treasure. The fact that all of these expeditions have returned empty-handed has not deterred others from chasing this will-of-the-wisp. The island has no native population and is owned by Costa Rica. Cocoanuts, palmettos, berries of many kinds and wild pigs constitute most of the available food supply to be found on the island.

Treasure hunters are romantic persons and enjoy the thrill of a treasure hunt even though they do not always find the treasure. Many kinds of "Doodle Bugs" have been tried out in the search for this treasure. Some of the expeditions have, however, gone about it in a more business-like way and tried to scoop the treasure up with steam shovels and scrapers. It was the custom in those days to shoot down the poor slaves that helped bury the treasure as dead men tell no tales. Those who are fortunate enough to find the treasure will, no doubt, find the bones of many dead "patrones" sprawled over the iron-bound chests stored away on Cocos Island.

LOST MINES AND BURIED TREASURE OF TUMACACORI MISSION

Very interesting history clusters about the Tumacacori Mission and the little settlement of Tubac, in the beautiful Santa Cruz valley, 22 miles from Nogales on the state highway to Tucson. This old mission is visited annually by more than 5,000 people from without the state of Arizona.

Among other interesting facts related of Tubac is that a military expedition commanded by Captain Juan Bautista Anza set forth from Tubac about 1784, marching under orders from higher military authority, to the Bay of San Francisco, and establishing there the Presidio, and naming the city of San Francisco. The first printing press brought into Arizona was set up at Tubac, and a newspaper called ''The Arizonan'' was conducted by Colonel Cross, a veteran of the Mexican War.

This once beautiful mission was the center of extensive mining operations carried on by the Spanish after Father Kino and his devoted Jesuit assistants began spreading the gospel in these parts. Old furnaces and slag dumps near the mission and caved in shafts and tunnels in the mountains indicate that operations were carried on for a great many years.

The rooms of the mission are vacant now and the bells have fallen from the tower. The padre sleeps beneath the altar and the happy voices of the Indian children have passed into silence forever. In those ancient and now almost mythical days the Cross and the Spanish Crown held joint and united sway over the entire region. It was in furtherance of their great work of proselyting the natives that the early fathers built those long chains of missions. For 300 years mines were developed and the flow of precious metals across the Sierra Madre to the capital, thence to Spain was regular and continuous.

The shadow of the Spanish Crown has passed away; the flag of Mexico has been moved southward, and the ruins of the Tumacacori Mission and the old mines lie under the protection of the peaceful American Eagle.

Dreams of gold and buried treasure have ever invaded the minds of men. So prospectors and adventurers dig for the gold and silver they imagine is hidden near the ancient ruins. Old documents now in existence claim that the mine called ''The Virgin Guadalupe'' belonged to Tumacacori. It measured one league from the big gate of the temple to the south and west; and from the waters of the San Roman, it measured 1800 varas to the north. In a southerly direction to the west there are two peaks torn down by powder being placed in the rocks. The signs remain blotted out and people could pass over these rocks treading on the values and never see them.

The enclosure is 50 varas square covering up the treasure inside and outside the mine. The gold and silver was brought from the Huachuca Mountains, 2050 burro loads of silver and 905 loads of gold and silver. The total value of the gold and silver amounts to 45 million pesos.

Follow straight ahead through the pass in the mountains to the south about three leagues from the Guadalupe mine. To the south of this pass runs a creek that passes by the old town of Santa Cruz. The mine is to the left of the pass. From the Guadalupe to this mine which is called the Pure Conception, it is three leagues. This mine has a tunnel 300 varas long that has the name of the Pure Conception cut in the rock over the mouth or door of the tunnel. The tunnel runs to the north and at a distance of about 200 varas they began to cut pure silver. In the face of this tunnel the metal is yellow and is one half silver ane one-fifth gold. Fifty varas from the mouth of the mine in a southerly direction will be found slabs of virgin silver weighing from 25 to 250 pounds each. This mine is covered by an iron door with copper handles.

Half way between the Guadalupe and the mine called Pure Conception, is the mine called The Opata. This mine has a tunnel 400 varas long running to the south. The metal in this mine is native silver and is found in caliche. From the south of this mine runs a long mesa in the direction of the setting sun.

From The Opata it is a league to the mine called Tumacacori. This mine is to the west and on the other side of the mountain. The crown and all the treasure belonging to the Saint Guadalupe, was left in this mine, Tumacacori. There is a copper box that has a key in one corner, there is a screw. Take out the screw and pull out the iron bar and open the box. There will be found all the maps of the great treasure.

The mine called San Pedro is a league and a half from the side of the temple to the west and when the sun is rising it strikes in the mouth of the tunnel. In this mine will be found deposits of virgin silver.

The mine called Isabella is one league to the north of the San Pedro. In this mine Isabella will be found deposits containing gold and silver. From the San Pedro a trail descends to the Guadalupe and then followed by a canyon to the south and reaches the spring of San Roman.

There are those who claim that a small part of this treasure was found in the seventeenth century by a Spanish lady and carried on mules to the City of Mexico. The lady could not rest or sleep until she had deposited the treasure in the house of the Spanish Viceroy at Mexico City. The lady soon thereafter ceased to breathe entirely as the Viceroy had her poisoned and kept the treasure for himself. However, she only recovered a small part of the great treasure and there should be plenty left to reward the searchers. As the old Mexican said to me about 20 years ago when he gave me the document, "It's all yours."

BURIED GOLD OF CASA GRANDE

In the year 544 the Toltecs abandoned Huhuetla-pallan, capital of the Kingdom of Tlapateca, situated in the northern regions. Guided by Huemec, their principal chief, they passed along the west coast and through what is now the State of Jalisco, Mexico, from where they crossed over the mountains to Toll-antzinco, where they remained until 645; then going to Tollan, ancient city of the Ottomies, situated 80 kilometers north of the city of Mexico, where they erected two pyramids, Tonacotecuhtili, to the sun, and Tezcatlicope, to the moon. They sacrificed every year five beautiful little girls to Tlaloc, the rain god. After a drouth and prolonged wars the Toltecs split up; one half going to the present site of Mexico City, and the other half to Central America, where they established the Kingdom of Copantl.

Many people believe that the old houses found along the Gila and Salt Rivers were built by the Tol-tecs and that this is the location of the ancient King-dom of Tlapalteca. The writer believes that this is an erroneous view and that the houses were built by the ancestors of the Papago and Pima Indians that lived in the valley during the reign of Montezuma. The In-dians call the old houses Casa Montezuma. The out-ward point of their chronology is Montezuma, and everything is dated from the time of that monarch. The fact that a labyrinth was found on the wall of the Casa Grande would indicate that it was built during the time of Montezuma. It is a well-known fact in Mexico that Montezuma's castles had a labyrinth in which the treasures were placed for safe keeping. Just how the knowledge of the labyrinth was brought from ancient Crete to the Aztecs in Mexico is unknown, unless it was brought over by the white men that visited the Aztec capital several times from the year 922 on for several years. This man stated that he and other men like himself had come from across the ocean from the orient.

When Francisco Vasquez Coronado, with 300 Spaniards and 800 Indians passed along the Gila River in 1540 searching for the Seven Cities of Cibola, he stated that the Indians of the Rio Gila and the upper valley of the Rio Del Norte were living in villages built of mud, mixed with certain balls of hard matter, and well cemented together. Their houses were generally four stories high, with no opening on the first floor, accessible only by movable ladders, with top terraces and an underground apartment, occupied exclusively by the men and used as estufas; in fact, similar in every respect to the existing pueblos of New Mexico, and the ruins of Casa Grande.

Padre Kino visited the ruins in 1694, coming to the Gila from the present site of Tumacacori Mission. The Indians told him of a large ruin to the north and accompanied by a few soldiers he found the casa in ruins, having been destroyed some time during the

Casa Grande Ruins Before Restoration, 1880

154 years that elapsed since Coronado passed along the Gila.

Lieutenant W. H. Emory visited the ruins in 1847 when he passed down the Gila River with the American army of the west, 307 years after Coronado had passed that way. There was a tradition among the Pimas at that time to the effect that "In bygone days a woman of surprising beauty resided in a green spot in the mountains near the valley. All the men admired and paid court to her. She received the tributes of their devotion, grain, skins, etc., but gave no love or other favor in return. Her virtue and her determination to remain unmarried were equally firm. There came a drouth which threatened the world with famine. In their distress the people applied to her, and she gave them corn from her stock, and the supply seemed to be endless. Her goodness was unbounded. Then one day as she lay asleep with her body exposed, a drop of rain fell on her stomach, which produced conception. A son was the issue, who was the founder of a new race which built all these houses.

No treasure of any importance, other than tomahawks and pottery, have ever been found in any of these old houses along the Gila and Salt Rivers. In 1520 when the Spaniards imprisoned Montezuma and demanded gold, runners were sent out from the capital to every part of the country advising the people to bury their treasures until the Spaniards had been driven from their country. This, according to tradition, was done. One of Montezuma's treasures was recently unearthed at Monte Alban, in the state of Michoacan, Mexico, and was valued at $25,000,000.

The great treasure that belonged to the Montezumas that built all these big houses in the Gila and Salt River valleys is stored in a cave in the Salt River Mountains near the Yaqui Indian village of Guadalupe.

THE JAMES BOYS' GOLD

When my mother was a young girl she went to school in Clay County, Missouri, with Frank and Jesse James, the famous Missouri outlaws. When I was about three years of age my family moved from Kit Carson's old stamping grounds in Kentucky to St. Joseph, Missouri. When we reached Quincy, Illinois, the James boys' were on the rampage, robbing and looting and shooting men, it was said, just to see them fall. Only three days before our arrival, it was reported, they had shot three men out of apple trees while riding along the road at breakneck speed with a six-shooter in each hand and the bridle reins in their teeth. An excited farmer trying to tell my father about the gang said six sheriffs went to Jesse's house to arrest him and old Jesse came out with a six-shooter in each hand and a knife in his teeth and killed all the officers before they could fire a single shot. A great many people were going down the east side of the Mississippi River in order to keep from crossing into Missouri from Quincy. Mother said she did not think the James boys' would bother us as she had known them in school before going to Kentucky. We crossed over the Mississippi and went on to St. Joseph without seeing any bandits that resembled the James boys'. However, we passed by Jesse's house out on Twenty-third street in St. Joseph but didn't know it at the time.

Jesse was killed soon after that by Bob Ford and I often heard father and mother talking about it. They, like many other people living nearby, drove down to see Jesse when he was dead. Mother said he did not look like Jesse James to her and many other people thought the same as she did, they did not care to say much about it for some reason unknown to me. Father once said it might have been some one else killed in order to give Jesse a chance to get away. Some years later a man living near us bought the old black horse that Jesse used to ride. He was an old horse then and had a white star in his forehead and several small spots on his sides which all the old-timers claimed were bullet marks. I used to ride the horse with other children and play war on him. He would lie flat on the ground with his head and neck stretched out like he was dead. Men that had known the bandit claimed he had trained the horse to do that.

It was rumored in that part of the country that after a Kansas bank robbery the gang crossed the Missouri River about 10 miles north of St. Joseph near a little town called Amazonia, where we had purchased a fruit farm and were living at that time. The bandits were being hard pressed by a posse and decided to bury the loot and take to the Missouri hills along the north side of the river. The gold was buried at the roots of an old oak tree that grew along the highway not far from our farm. This old tree had several hundred bullet holes in it and it was said that it was used as a target by Frank and Jesse James, Jim and Cole Younger and Emmet Dalton, who would ride around

the tree with their bridle reins in their teeth and
shoot at it while their horses were running at full
speed.

When about 12 years of age I felt as mother had
gone to school with Frank and Jesse when they were
boys, and as I had been riding Jesse's horses, I was
therefore qualified to look for the loot. We had a
colored man working for us on the farm taking care
of the fruit trees. This old negro was known to us as
Uncle Mose. His wife had died some years before,
leaving him a son about my own age. This boy was
called Little Mose, and he was very fond of o'possum
meat cooked with sweet potatoes and for that reason
he never overlooked an opportunity to go coon or
o'possum hunting with the white boys in the neigh-
borhood. We had six coon and o'possum hounds that
had been sent to us from our old home in Kentucky.

One dark night when a light rain was falling we
decided to go out and dig up the James boys' gold.
Little Mose, ever alert for a chance to go o'possum
hunting, suggested that we take the hounds along and
in case we didn't dig up the money we could go o'possum hunting. Our equipment consisted of a pick and
shovel and several strong sacks to carry the money
home in. We started out along a rail fence that en-
closed a cornfield beyond which was a thick patch of
timber through which ran a small stream full of frogs
and fish, an ideal place to jump a coon or o'possum.

The six dogs were scouting far ahead and the little
colored boy was staying close to us. Every time one

of the hounds barked Mose said he was barking at a
ghost, as he had never heard the dogs bark that way
before. He kept this up until he had all of the other
boys thinking the same way he did, and by the time
we arrived at the old oak tree we could see Jesse
James' ghost looking at us from behind almost every
tree and out of every fence corner.

After due consideration we decided that a smart
man like Jesse James would certainly bury his loot
in a well-known place so he would be able to come
back later and find it without any trouble and that
the old oak tree was without a doubt the place to look
for it. Mose said it was on the south side as it was
bad luck to bury anything on the north side of a tree.
That sounded reasonable to the assembled treasure
hunters, so we spudded in on the south side of the
tree and after reaching a depth of about three feet
without finding any money, we thought Mose might
be mistaken and that we had better dig on the north
side of the tree. After putting down four holes on
as many sides of the tree without finding anything,
we sat down to rest and discuss future operations,
when the dogs, by their peculiar manner of barking,
indicated to us that they had treed something; so we
all rushed over to see what it was. We found the
dogs barking up an old elm tree that was full of
squirrel nests and out on one limb about half way up
the tree could be seen a big fat o'possum. We started
to throw chunks of rotten wood trying to dislodge it
and every time one of these chunks hit the ground the
dogs would pounce upon it, thinking it was the o'pos-

sum that had fallen out of the tree. Mose got impatient and suggested that we let him go up and shake the o'possum out. So we boosted him up and he got out on a limb under the o'possum and was trying to shake him loose when he stepped on a small limb that broke under his weight and let him fall. The dogs were alert and ready to jump on anything that fell, so the instant that Mose struck the ground the dogs were all on top of him, with about half of them holding his shirt and the other half had him by the pants. About two jerks and the little fellow was completely undressed and yelling for us to get him out. By the time we pulled the dogs off, little Mose was in bad shape. One of the other boys climbed the tree and shook the o'possum out and gave it to Mose.

On the way back to the treasure we heard a scream over toward the other side of the timber and Mose said it was a panther screaming like a woman in distress in order to get us to go over there so it could eat us up. Not having any desire to be eaten up just then, we took a short cut for home over a trail that took us past an old house occupied by Abe Richhart, an old wood-chopper. The dogs were now trailing something across on the other side of the field from us and by the time we reached old Abe's house the dogs were coming down across the yard about 10 feet behind a black panther. There was a large hole under the house and the panther and dogs were all headed for it.

Old Abe, standing out on the porch with nothing on but his night shirt, saw the panther go under the house and he tried to stop up the hole with a large circular saw that was standing against a cherry tree in the yard. About the time he had the saw ready to close up the hole out came the panther and all the dogs and knocked Abe down with the saw, the panther and all the dogs on top of him. By the time we succeeded in getting Abe out he had lost his night shirt and was scratched from head to foot. The dogs killed the panther and the next day all the farmers came to see it and said it was the largest panther that had ever been killed in that country. Mose and his dad cooked the o'possum in a large Dutch oven with a lot of sweet potatoes until it was nice and brown and said that it was the best o'possum meat that they had ever tasted.

The James boys' gold, if it ever was there, is still out there under the old oak tree.

THE GREAT TREASURE

There is a tradition among the Papago Indians that a great treasure lies buried northwest of Tucson along the Silver Bell road in the vicinity of the little town of Red Rock. In ancient times the valley was densely populated by people who made their living by tilling the soil. They worked the rich mines that abounded in the nearby mountains to obtain gold and silver with which to adorn themselves.

As the years passed, a large amount of treasure was accumulated and worked into ornaments of odd and quaint designs.

In the tenth century a small number of white men appeared in the valley and established themselves among the Indians with whom they bartered for gold and silver. These strange men were armed with long spears and swords and carried crosses made of metal. They dressed in clothing made of cloth, which indicated that they had come from the east with other men like themselves. They made many trips into the surrounding country to barter for gold and taught the Indians many useful occupations. Often some of them would be gone for months on these trips and a large amount of gold and silver would be accumulated. Several years passed and then one day a large band of hostile Indians from the north swooped down into the valley and killed them all. The gold and silver had been buried and was never found. Some years ago the spears, swords and metal crosses were recovered from a bed of caliche near a deserted lime kiln. The formation incrusted relics could not have formed in less than eight or nine hundred years time.

These white men are now believed to have been a band of Phoenician sailors that had been ship-wrecked and landed on the Atlantic coast or a party of Norsemen from the colony established on the coast of Maine by Lief Eriscon in the tenth century. There was a Christian man on the ship with Eric the Red when he left Norway for Iceland. This same man is supposed to have been with Lief and Thorvald when they landed on the coast of Maine to establish their colony. There is an Aztec legend that a white man visited their capital in the year 922 and stated that he had come from the Orient with other white men like himself. This man made several trips to the Aztec capital and then disappeared in the year 935 during the reign of Mitl. This white man was known to the Indians as Quetzalcoatl.

Many ancient ruins can still be seen in the valley around Red Rock and the old Papagoes still gather around their campfires and talk about the great treasure buried there by Quetzalcoatl.

MAXIMILIAN'S GOLD

In the year 1866 a pack train consisting of 18 mule loads of gold bullion, guarded by a captain and 25 soldiers, was started from the gold mines in the Yaqui Indian country, Southern Sonora, to the City of Mexico.

The gold was consigned to Maximilian, Emperor of Mexico. Gold was at that time being collected from every available source to bolster up the tottering throne of the young Emperor. The French had withdrawn their troops and revolution had broken out in every part of the country. The young Empress Carlota had gone to France to plead with Napoleon III for help.

The pack train was traveling east from the Yaqui country, making for a crossing on the Mayo River near El Rancho Santa Barbara, where they hoped to strike the trail that led through the Chinipas Pass and down to the City of Mexico. Upon arrival at the Mayo, the captain was informed that revolution had broken out in that part of the country and that Chato Almada, with a large number of his macheteres, was in the vicinity of the crossing.

Anticipating an attack, the captain buried the 18 mule loads of gold and then moved on to a distance of one kilometer to the crossing, where he camped for the night. Almada discovered the camp and attacked it during the night. All the soldiers with the exception of two were killed. These two jumped into the swift stream and made their escape in the darkness.

Almada was unable to locate the gold, believing it had been thrown into the river.

Long after Maximilian had been captured at Queretaro and executed with Miramon and Mejia at Cerro de las Campanas, the two soldiers returned to the Mayo crossing to search for the buried gold. The river had overflown many times and the landscape was so changed that they were never able to locate the place where they had years before helped to bury the 18 mule loads.

Mexico is a land of ghost stories, and the natives at El Rancho Santa Barbara say that on dark, windy nights, the old captain and his 23 soldiers rise from their graves, mount their mules and gallop over the field where millions of dollars is buried, and then vanish into the darkness, as suddenly as they came.

LOST PEG-LEG MINE

The Peg-Leg Mine is another one of the West's mythical mines. On account of its great richness and inaccessability, located as it is, in the heart of a great desert, the Peg-Leg Mine has a tremendous appeal for those looking for a man size job. The stories told of the search for this lost mine breathe the spirit of the west's hardy sons.

Peg-Leg Smith was an argonaut in the gold rush in California in 1849. The Peg-Leg gold mine is a tradition involved in various interpretations and it is difficult to say just where it was really located, but out in the desert country of Eastern California, is perhaps its true location.

Peg-Leg Smith, a contemporary of Jim Bridger, Kit Carson, Bill Williams and many others, followed the pursuits of the frontiersman-trapper, trader, scout and miner. He rode back and forth over the Golden West and his life was replete with thrilling episodes of romance and adventure. He ranged over the mountains and boundless plains from the Platte to the Pacific, and if we are to believe the stories told of him, many a savage redskin bit the dust at the crack of his trusty rifle.

One day Peg-Leg and another man set out from Yuma on foot supposedly headed for Los Angeles, but probably stalking one of the numerous Indians who brought gold and cashed it at Yuma. Many had tried to get these Indians to tell them where they found this gold. The Indians refused to tell, so men would follow them to try and locate the place, always losing the Indians near the Cottonwood Springs in San Bernardino County.

Days later Peg-Leg was picked up, near Walker's Station on the Southern Pacific, dying of thirst and hunger. He was taken to a hospital in Los Angeles where he died without telling the location of the place where he found a large black nugget of gold that was on his person. All information relative to the place was garnered from his ravings before death overtook him.

His partner fell from exhaustion, but Peg-Leg kept on after finding a small hill covered with black rocks. The black nugget was one of these rocks, and had come from the tallest of three little hills which the two men had climbed to get their bearings. The hill had a black summit, but was a chalky yellow around its base.

The Peg-Leg Mine is somewhere between Walker's Station and Warner's Pass and is located north of Cottonwood Springs.

THE BRADY MINES

Seventy-five years ago a remarkable young man, Peter Rainsford Brady, came out of the east into the Rio Grande country, then as now, the Texas Frontier. He was remarkable from the fact that through the years of his life he held the unquestioned leadership among men when forced by circumstances to act as a real leader in a wilderness where the only highways were Indian trails. Meeting and dealing with all manner of men, good and bad, Whites, Mexicans, and Indians, of numerous tribes and traits of character. His word was his bond, his code of honor the law of the desert.

Owning and operating during his business career, two of Arizona's richest mines. He never posed as a great mining authority, but accepted what measure of prosperity he derived from his mining activities as the result of his labors rather than the result of his wisdom. His losses he accepted as the consequences of his mistakes and lack of mining knowledge, candidly acknowledged the fact and blamed no other for them.

Mr. Brady was a native of the District of Columbia, born in Washington, August 4th, 1825. His education was secured at Georgetown College, Georgetown, D. C., and he made his entry into the more serious duties of life as a midshipman appointed to the United

States Sloop-of-War "Plymouth" in 1843, when 18 years of age. In 1845 he left the United States Coast Survey to go to Texas, drawn by the prospect of war with Mexico. In 1846 he joined Captain W. G. Crump's Company of Texas Rangers, in command of Colonel P. H. Bell, and served on the frontier until the close of the Mexican war. He was living in Jalisco, Mexico, when James Marshall discovered gold in California, and started the great gold rush over the Santa Fe Trail.

Returning to Texas he again served in the Rangers until 1853, when he started westward in charge of the expedition of Colonel Andrew B. Gray, to survey the first Pacific railroad from Indianola, Texas, to San Diego, California, and known as the Memphis-El Paso and San Diego Railroad. The trip occupied seven months, and while in Arizona he met and made a firm and lifelong friend of a semi-civilized Papago Indian, Juan Gradillo, who gave him such valuable information on the great Ajo copper deposits that he organized in San Francisco in July, 1854, the first mining company to operate in Arizona, he then returned to take possession of the old Ajo mine near the Mexican border. Thereafter Mr. Brady lived continuously in Arizona, occupied at different times in mining, farming, milling and prospecting. He was twice a member of the legislative council, serving in 1857 and again in 1891.

It was while Mr. Brady was engaged in farming at Florence, Arizona, in 1869, that Juan Gradillo, making a trip from Sonora, Mexico, to Florence, to visit

Guerari Mission Near Nogales, 1691 A. D.

the friend whom he had respected for twenty-five years, found and brought to Florence, the rich float from the Vekol mine and induced Mr. Brady to locate the first claim, thereby creating a record for himself as the pioneer owner and operator of two of Arizona's greatest mines—Ajo among the coppers and Vekol in the list of silver mines.

Mr. Brady's company, the Arizona Mining and Trading Company mined the rich glance and carbonate ores at Ajo, and freighted them to Yuma and down the Colorado River by steamer to Port Isabelle on the Gulf of California. These steamers were under command of Captain Isaac Polhamus who was at that time Master of Transportation for the old Colorado River Steamboat, or Transportation Company. Capt. Polhamus is one of Arizona's oldest and finest characters.

From Port Isabelle the ore was shipped by ocean vessels to Swansea, Wales, the company waiting from twelve to eighteen months for their returns on the ore. Mr. Brady and the little group of men associated with him, were the only white men in all the Great Southwest between the Utah State line and the Mexican boundary, and from New Mexico to Yuma on the Colorado River and California State line.

While Mr. Brady, Granville Oury and others were operating the mine at Ajo, a party of 500 Mexican soldiers headed by the Prefect of Caborca, Sonora, attacked the mine early one morning about daylight and demanded the delivery of the mine, claiming it was owned by the Mexicans. The boundary line under the Gadsden purchase had not yet been established, and the Mexicans threatened to take the mine by force if it was not surrendered within two hours. The Americans had built a small fort on top of a little hill near a spring and just south of the mine. There were two entrances to the fort, one on the north end and the other in the south. The American force consisted of Brady, Oury and ten or twelve others. The men were ordered to march out at the north end and come around the hill to the south entrance and keep it up until it looked to the Mexicans like they were going to encounter a large force of Americans. Tired from having marched all the way across the desert from Sonoyta without water, they decided to hold a parley. They asked the Americans to allow them to come in and water their horses and themselves and were told by Brady that they could come in two at a time, stating that if he allowed them to come all at once he would not be able to hold his men. After watering their stock the Mexicans headed for Caborca and never stopped until they reached the Sonoyta River thirty-seven miles to the south. Mr. Brady was a strong man physically and mentally, and of unquestioned integrity. A gentleman of the old school, he was genial, kind and hospitable. He passed away on the 2nd day of May, 1902, at the age of 77 years, leaving a fine family and a host of friends throughout the Southwest to mourn his loss.

LOST SQUAW MINE

The story of the Lost Squaw Mine has been told all over the Southwest. Many years ago two Yuma bucks and an old squaw, while traveling over the Indian trail between Phoenix and Yuma picked up a piece of very rich gold ore and took it home with them. It was only a piece of float that had become detached from a vein and the Indians had no idea where it came from. The ore was shown to some Mexicans who became interested in the rich specimen and engaged the squaw to take them to the spot where she had found it. She led them to the spot and told them they would have to locate the mine themselves. The Mexicans were unable to find the mine and beat and threatened to kill the old squaw because she would not take them to it. The squaw escaped at night and refused to take anyone else to the place where she had found the wonderful ore. The two bucks had been killed and the old squaw was the only one left that knew the secret.

A great many people tried to find the Lost Squaw Mine; among them was Ed Shefflin, the discoverer of Tombstone. Ed located the squaw but was unable to persuade her to take him to the place where she years before picked up the rich float. However, she gave Shefflin information that enabled him to find the place and after making several unsuccessful attempts to find the mine Shefflin gave up the search.

Some years later while in San Francisco Shefflin read in the newspapers of a rich discovery of gold ore having been made in the Harqua Halas and declared it to be the Lost Squaw Mine. He returned to Arizona and after looking the mine over found it to be just as the old squaw had described the location to him. She had taken the Mexicans to within a few hundred yards of what afterward proved to be the great Harqua Hala that produced many millions in gold and was one of the richest mines in Arizona.

Ed Shefflin made a half million dollars in Tombstone and many years later died with his boots on at Coffee Creek, Douglas County, Oregon. The last entry in his dairy stated, "Struck it at last." Some rich ore samples were lying nearby but the mine has not been located.

LEGEND OF DR. THORNE MINE RECALLS ORIGIN OF SQUAW TEA

Many years ago, so the story goes, old Doctor Thorne was captured by the Apache Indians. History or legend is not very explicit as to just how or when this occurred. However, most of the pioneers knew Dr. Thorne and were familiar with the history of his trips into the Superstition and Four Peaks country in search of the wonderful mine said to have been shown to him by the Indians.

Years after Thorne had been captured by the Indians, there came a drought which threatened the country with famine. Palo Verde and mesquite beans were scarce and wild game had drifted away in search of grass. All the Apache warriors and young men were out making a living, and according to history they were not very particular as to how they made it. Ranches were raided, pioneers killed and cattle and horses driven off.

While the bucks were away on these raids a terrible disease broke out among the squaws and papooses. No one seemed to know just what the disease was or how it started. At any rate, the squaws were in great distress with a breaking out all over their bodies and were beginning to look like the devil.

The Apache medicine man was working overtime trying to concoct a cure; daily he boiled roots and bark into a strong tea; hit a mesquite tree three times with his tomahawk and blew the smoke from his macoochie cigarette into the air to see if the signs were right for a cure. The wind always blew the wrong direction.

The squaws were desperate and appealed to the white man for help. Dr. Thorne gathered some green twigs from a plant that grows profusely all over the state of Arizona and many parts of the west. This he boiled into a strong tea and after giving the squaws a generous helping he took them down to the Salt River and had them scrubbed from head to foot with a horse brush which knocked off most of the bumps and started them on the road to recovery. A wonderful change came over the squaws and "every day in every way" they improved until finally when the bucks came home and found them all dressed in bright new calico dresses and their hair combed and each with a skin that they liked to touch, they were so pleased by the wonderful transformation that they immediately decided to call a pow-wow and have Dr. Thorne released. The matter was mentioned to Mangus Coloradas and he said, "La-Hoit-Ma-Coop," which translated into English means "You said it, kid."

From that day until this the weed from which Doc boiled the magic medicine is called Squaw Tea.

Upon being released Thorne made his way to Santa Fe, New Mexico. Here he told a tale of finding a rich placer mine while he was a captive among the

Indians. A party of men was formed and went with Thorne to look for this rich placer, but were run out by the Indians.

Dr. Thorne next went to St. Louis and told his story to a newspaperman who printed it. Enough money was subscribed to keep him looking for a number of years, but he never could locate the place.

His money having given out he moved to the Rio Grande country of New Mexico where he finally died, but he left his story behind him.

According to Dr. Thorne he had been captured in the late 50's and was with the Indians until after the '60's. With his skill as a physician and surgeon and his knowledge of healing herbs he had won his life from torture and death. The Indians held him in high esteem, but would not turn him loose.

In the dead of winter when the Apaches were hard pressed for food and harder pressed by enemies Dr. Thorne became snow-blind. The tribe at that time was somewhere in the White Mountains. In the course of their travel they camped at a little stream that Dr. Thorne afterward said was between thirty and forty miles from the Black River. On the bare flat rock bottom of this stream Dr. Thorne found a yellow metal which he took to be gold. The Apaches noticed his interest in the "Pesh-la-chi"—yellow metal—so to lull their suspicions he told them that it was no good.

Before leaving Dr. Thorne located the place in his mind by observing landmarks, but suffering badly from snow-blindness his perspective was not so good. The camp was near an old stone corral which was an old structure according to the Indians. From the camp he could see "Sombrero Butte" and the "Sierra Pintadas," and located the camp as being between them. On leaving the camp the journey was south, and the trail crossed Salt River near its junction with the White River.

A. F. Banta and a man named Cooley looked for the mine in 1869. They received their information from Dr. Thorne himself. Banta was of the opinion that the mine was on Tonto Creek near the old ruins of Totonteac and the placer gold was only iron pyrites which he found in the stream there. Others disagree and think the mine located on the east side of Sombrero Butte and in the foothills of the White Mountains. The latter are probably right as Dr. Thorne saw the same place Banta speaks of, but did not identify it as the place. Dr. Thorne could not remember whether the Butte was on his right or left side as he journeyed south.

Dr. Thorne to the day of his death protested that he had found gold and that the richest mine in the west lay concealed in the hills to the north of Salt River.

THE MINES OF NEW MEXICO

The Mines of New Mexico were probably first mentioned in a historical way in the report of Francisco Sanchez Chamuscado, after the expedition of Troy Rodriguez and his companions in the year 1581. Soldiers were sent along with this religious expedition because it was stated that there were mines abounding with the precious metals in the region which they intended to visit.

Antonio De Espejo made his way up the Rio Grande in 1582 and visited the ancient pueblos of Acoma, Zuni and Moqui. With some Moqui guides he journeyed for forty-five leagues over a mountainous country, he found the mines and with his own hands obtained rich samples of silver ore.

According to Bandelier mining on a large scale did not begin in New Mexico until 1725. The great copper mine at Santa Rita started to work about 1800 on a large scale, but the Spaniards had gophered on it for years before. The metal was transported to Mexico City, a distance of over 1,000 miles, by pack mules and wagons, 100 mules, carrying 300 pounds each, being constantly employed.

Traditions speak of numerous and productive mines having been in operation in Mexico, Arizona, and New Mexico before the expulsion of the Spaniards in 1680; but that the Indians, seeing that the cupidity of the conquerors was the cause of their cruel oppressions, determined to conceal all the mines by filling them up, and obliterating all traces of them. They did their work well, for after the second conquest (the Spaniards doing very little mining for a number of years), succeeding generations only found a very few through accident.

It is generally credited by both the Spanish and white population of the west that the Indians, up to the present day, are acquainted with the locations of a large number of these mines, of which they jealousy guard the secret.

The old chiefs and medicine men warn the Indians against discovering the mines to the whites or Spaniards. The Indian who reveals the location of these hidden treasures will surely perish by the wrath of their gods.

PLANCHAS DE PLATA

The world famous Planchas De Plata Silver Mine was discovered about 1730 in the Magdelena district, only a short distance south of the international boundary and within easy distance of Nogales. The name signifies plates or balls of silver, and the original discovery was literally of that nature. Large balls and plates of native silver varying in size from a marble up to that of a washtub were found in great profusion.

J. F. Velasco, who published a book upon Sonora mines, in 1850, relates that one chunk was found that was so large that it was too heavy for a single mule to pack, and with the tools then attainable it could not be cut up. So a carriage, swung from the backs of two mules, was arranged and the silver nugget hoisted to the limb of a tree by means of ropes. The mules were driven underneath and the precious cargo was lowered upon the carriage. In that way it was conveyed the entire distance to the City of Mexico. Many years after this discovery, a silver nugget totaling in weight 2700 pounds was discovered in that vicinity by American prospectors and soldiers who were dispatched from Mexico City to force the Americans to abandon the mine. Similar deposits were found by the Jesuit priests in the vicinity of the Tumacacori Mission and only a short distance north of Planchas de Plata. Tradition has it that 45 million pesos in gold and silver bars were buried in the Guadalupe mine near the ruins of the ancient mission.

The Arizona range of mountains which contains the famous district of mines, known as the Planchas de Plata, is by no means a recent discovery. That these mines existed and were worked by the Spaniards is a fact well authenticated in the archives of Spain and Mexico.

In the year 1835, Mr. Ward, Minister of the British Government to Mexico, made a special report of this district to his Government. An old Spanish work, entitled "The Zealous Apostles of the Society of Jesus," (pp. 232 to 237, Vol. II, Chap. II), has the following regarding the discoveries of the Planchas de Plata: "There was discovered in 1769, in the Apache frontier, in the region known as "La Arizona" to the north of the Presidio of Altar, and distant from there forty leagues, in the vicinity of Aqua Caliente, a region of native silver. A Yaqui Indian made the discovery and showed it to a trader who made the discovery public. Pieces of silver weighing from 1 to 50 pounds were found at a depth of a few varas. Afterward, other pieces were found weighing 500 pounds, and one piece weighing 3,500 pounds. This find soon brought together a large number of people who excavated the earth in different directions. Some found smaller chunks, than those above mentioned, others merely grains of silver and others found nothing.

The foregoing is also cited in the statistics of the State of Sonora, "Jose Francisco Valesco, Mexico, 1850," (p. 190) contains the following:

"From the foregoing you can easily understand

that this important placer of pure silver has its origin from some very rich vein or ledge which must exist in the neighboring mountains because all of them contain more or less mineral. The truth of this discovery is not only authenticated in the history to which I have referred but also in 'Las Ocias Espanolas' and in the writings of the archives of the missions of "Pimeria Alta."

It is said that the military commander of the Presidio of Altar in 1769, gathered the silver in large masses claiming it as a treasure that appertained to the King and accounted to him for what he had done. The interested parties made reclamation, but failed to obtain a favorable response, they then had recourse to the tribunal of Guadalajara who referred it to the courts of Madrid. Seven years later the King decided that this silver belonged to his royal domain, and that they had only worked for his sole benefit, etc.

Due to the despoliation that was pursued by the King and to the threats of hostile Apache Indians the region was depopulated until about the year 1879. An expedition headed by Don Dionisio Robles visited the region in 1817, but had to retire because of the Indians. Many who took part in this expedition asserted that the whole region is one mass of mines and that there is a range to the east of this point from whence came large quantities of silver and where they found many veins of gold and silver. The mine, "Ojitas de San Roman," which is a little further north was also rich according to Don Teodoro Salazar.

THE LOST YUMA MINE

The "Yuma" Mine is one of the numerous "Lost Mines" in which the history of Arizona is so prolific, but there is a solid foundation on which to work.

A number of years ago an officer of the army was cashiered for some crime, and in consequence of the attendant disgrace came to the west. He adopted the name of "Yuma," by which name he was known to his acquaintances in Arizona.

"Yuma's" name was Thomas McLain, a graduate of West Point. He came west to California in 1849, and located in Mariposa County, but through a chain of circumstances was forced to leave. He then came into Arizona where Mr. Charles O. Brown, who had known him in California, recognized him on the streets of Tucson in 1858.

Yuma carried on a trade with the Apaches from his ranch in the Papago country west of Tucson. He also ran a herd of 500 cattle on this ranch. Taking out supplies of calico, beads, ammunition, and such articles as the Indians coveted, he would meet them on the summit of the Pinal Mountains and trade.

After gaining the confidence of the Indians, they showed him a marvelously rich gold mine near the trading place, from which they took the metal that they traded to him. It was a blind lead, and after extracting all they wanted, the Indians would carefully cover it with earth, gravel, and brush, so that no traces of its existence would be betrayed. The Indians exacted a promise from ''Yuma'' not to divulge its location, nor to show it to any other white man.

On his last trip, in 1860, he was accompanied by General Walker, afterwards agent of the Papagos. After trading with the Indians they set out for Tucson, and on their way visited the mine. They easily found the mine; scraped off the loose earth with tin plates and broke the sparkling quartz with their hatchets. Filling their saddle bags, they hurriedly replaced the earth and brush and hurried to Tucson for fear the Indians would find them out and exact vengeance.

They showed the quartz to the public at Tucson. Charles O. Brown, Grant Oury, Wm. S. Oury, Hiram S. Stevens, Samuel Hughes, and A. Lazard all saw the ore, and vouched for the authenticity of the tale, and description of the ore. The ore was so studded with gold that a pin head could not touch the quartz between the beads of the yellow metal.

The hunt for the El Dorado was put off due to an outbreak of the Apaches. Page was killed at Canada de Oro and the Apaches raided to the city limits of Tucson.

Old ''Yuma'' went out to gather and drive his cattle into Tucson. The Papagos killed him, because they feared he was planning a raid on them with the Apaches. They took clubs and beat out his brains while he was asleep. The cattle had been gathered up during the morning. At noon "Yuma" laid down under a mesquite to rest and fell asleep. It was then that the Papagoes killed him.

The secret was then the sole possession of General Walker, but the continued Indian war precluded his using the knowledge. Being a feeble man, he succumbed to consumption in 1865. Before dying he gave directions to John Sweeney, his blacksmith roommate, but Sweeney's brain was in a muddled condition from drink, and he naturally got things mixed. Sweeney told Charles O. Brown all he knew of the locality, and as Sweeney died shortly afterwards in Florence, Brown had the only knowledge of the mine. He searched, but could not find it.

The mine must be situated close to the junction of the Gila and San Pedro Rivers as "Yuma" had his principal trading station at this point. This was before any white settlers were in that part of the country and was as near as he could get with his wagons. He used pack animals to trade with tribes too far away to come to his station. While at this station "Yuma" would go off in company with some Indians, allowing no one else to accompany him, and after an absence of one and a half to two days, would return loaded down with white quartz full of gold. He often told that he went down the Gila, tied the horses up and climbed to the mine on foot, but General Walker was the only one who really could have given landmark locations after the death of "Yuma."

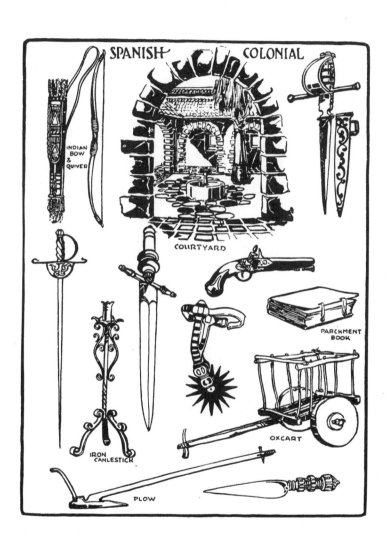

SPANISH COLONIAL

INDIAN BOW & QUIVER

COURTYARD

PARCHMENT BOOK

IRON CANLESTICK

OXCART

PLOW

LOST SQUAW HOLLOW MINE

In 1864, Judge J. T. Alsap, in company with other pioneers and under command of Colonel Woolsey, whose Indian fighting proclivities were familiar to all old-timers in Arizona, were engaged in one of the Apache conflicts so frequent about that time. After defeating the Indians about ten of the men prospected in close proximity to the camp and battle ground— known as "Squaw Hollow." Their efforts were rewarded, for in a few hours the prospectors returned with their hats full of a rich gold-bearing quartz it was ever the luck of the Judge to view. The Apache warriors of the conflict just past, were not satisfied altogether, and made a second call greatly augmented in numbers, and the Colonel and his followers found it necessary to retire and live to fight again.

Those who participated in the affair soon afterwards became widely separated, and seeking to keep the matter a secret, in order to return later, the find received no publicity. The Judge was satisfied in his own mind that the place had never been found since the first discovery as there were no prospect holes or mines in the basin. He searched the place several times, using Camp Creek as a base, but never located the rich mine.

The Judge may have been wrong as an old sheepherder told in later years of camping with a man in

"Squaw Hollow" during the '80's. This man was working a mine and bringing the ore to his cabin on the creek in the basin. The outlaw, for such he was, ground up and panned the rock at the cabin. The outlaw later sent the gold to his son who was attending a college in the East (Yale sounded like the place to the sheep-herder).

The sheep-herder never learned the name of the man, and on returning to the basin in later years did not find him there. Having no interest in mines the sheep-herder did not look for it, but remembered and told about the outlaw and his mine to another person, whom he was friendly with, on learning that this person was interested in mines.

LOST ADAM'S DIGGINGS

The search for the famous Adams Diggings has cost the lives of more men than any other lost mine in the great Southwest. Adams searched for years to relocate this fabulously rich placer mine which he and one other man had been forced to abandon and flee for their lives by a band of blood-thirsty Apache Indians that had swooped down from the mountains on their camp and murdered the other six members of the party that were operating the rich diggings.

From a letter of Robert T. Emmet, then 2nd Lt. of Ninth Cav., U. S. A. Dated March 5th, 1882.

Excerpts from letter are as follows:

"Nearly twenty years ago a man named Adams with seven others came from California into Arizona prospecting. They stopped at Camp Apache for rations and continued east. A few days march from Apache they found a great deal of gold in a small canyon. One of the men, a German, after working about ten days, became alarmed about the Indians and left, carrying about ten or twelve thousand dollars in gold as a result of his labor. This is shown by the books of the Post Trade at Fort Yuma who bought the gold from him.

"The remainder of the party built a cabin and continued work till rations were low, when all but two,

Adams and another man, started back to Camp Apache for supplies. The gold they had already mined was buried under the floor of the cabin.

"Adams and his companion waited till they thought the others should have returned when becoming quite alarmed at their long absence, they started in search of them.

"Looking back from the mountains on which they were climbing they saw the cabin in flames and their comrades, who had come in from another direction being massacred by the Indians. They concealed themselves till after dark and escaped."

Adams and the "Dutchman" had only the clothes on their backs, one pistol and a few rounds of ammunition. They headed south and lived on game they managed to kill with the one pistol. After wandering around for about ten days they were found in an exhausted condition on the headwaters of the Gila River, by a scouting party from Fort West. The Fort, now abandoned, is on the Gila River, north and west about 25 miles from Silver City. The mine is located north of the Fort and probably up near the headwaters of the Prieto (Black) River.

The man who escaped with Adams was killed in Texas by a herd of cattle. Adams was still living at the time the above letter was written.

Lieutenant W. H. Emory, in his Notes of a Military Reconnoissance from Fort Leavenworth in Kansas to

San Diego in California, which was published in 1848, states: "The Prieto (Black) River flows down from the mountains freighted with gold. Its sands are said to be full of this precious metal. A few adventurers who ascended the river hunting beaver washed the sands at night when they halted and were richly rewarded for their trouble. Tempted by their success, they made a second trip and were attacked and most of them killed by the Indians. My authority for this statement is Landeau, who, though an illiterate man, is truthful."

Shortly after being rescued Adams was reported to have stolen an army horse, two revolvers and other equipment one dark night and before leaving camp killed several Indian prisoners that were in the band that had attacked the Adams party at the mine. Adams became a fugitive from justice for 20 years and finally, when at liberty to go where he pleased, he tried to find his way back to his old diggings and spent the rest of his life looking for the fabulously rich mine and the $60,000 in gold dust and nuggets buried in the cabin that was burned by the Indians.

From the map left by Lieutenant Emory, giving the location on the head-waters of the Gila River where Adams and his partner were picked up, it would seem to indicate that the mine is located up toward the head-waters of the Black River and could be found without much trouble.

Some of the many expeditions that have gone into the White Mountains in search of the mine have used old Fort Wingate, in New Mexico, as their headquarters. On account of the small number of men in each expedition that went in search of the mine and owing to the fact that the Apaches were continually on the warpath at that time, a large number of men lost their lives.

Adams died at the age of 93 years and the wonderful mine and $60,000 in gold nuggets is still out there somewhere in the White Mountains and the Prieto (Black) River still flows down from the mountains freighted with gold.

The description, by Adams, of the mine should be helpful. The burned cabin was on the side of a narrow gulch, near an old stone corral in which the horses were kept. The sluice boxes were directly in front of the cabin and the flow of water to operate them was large. Pine timber, from which the boxes were made was plentiful, although the area was not heavily timbered.

Due to the fact that the Dr. Thorne Mine was located near an old stone corral some searchers for the mine contend that the Dr. Thorne Mine and the Lost Adams Diggings are one and the same. The old stone corral had no other evidence of man near it when found by Dr. Thorne. The Adams party used the corral for their horses, but to my knowledge knew of no other buildings, but their own cabin near the mine.

THE MINER EXPEDITION

The Miner Expedition was organized in Nevada to search for a lost placer digging in Arizona. In May, 1871, it left Prescott for Phoenix, intending to go to Old Fort Grant. When it left Prescott the party numbered about thirty. At Phoenix the party increased in numbers; some came from Florence, some from Tucson, and some from Sonora, so that when the party left Old Fort Grant they numbered about 267 men and were divided into five companies. They marched across to the San Pedro, thence to the mouth of the San Carlos, up that stream to its head, and then to Salt River where they prospected a few days. From there they went to the Tonto Basin and then to the mouth of Cherry Creek where they camped for some time, then to the Sierra Ancha Mountains where they prospected without finding either gold or silver. They finally returned to Cherry Creek Valley and down to Salt River across to some "wheatfields," and then to Pinto Creek where the company separated. The Prescott company returning to Prescott. Governor Safford and party went back to Tucson. There were a number of noted mining men in the company: Ed G. Peck, Al. Sieber, Willard Rive, R. W. Groom and others.

The expedition was undertaken in consequence of stories told by a man named Miner who acted as guide. He claimed that while out in that region with a party, one of the men, from a shovel full of earth panned out seventeen ounces of gold, and that he could lead the party to the place. He failed to do so and his story was believed to be false. Thus the largest expedition ever formed in Arizona to search for the precious metals came to nothing.

As the party from Phoenix came along the trail toward home, a small sharp butte was observed along the trail. One of the party in jest, said: "There is Miner's Needle!" Since that time the small sharp peak, which is located on the south side of the Superstitions and to the north of Bark's Ranch, has been known as "Miner's Needle." Miner was depending on a lone sharp peak to identify the placer ground.

"Weaver's Needle," sometimes called Sombrero Butte was named after Pauline Weaver who was the first man to observe and call attention to it. When Weaver first saw the large needle, he was scout and guide for a party chasing Indians with stolen horses. The party caught up with the Apaches, but did not get their horses back.

The Miner Expedition passed over and prospected near some of the richest mines developed in Arizona in later years.

The "Miner" Expedition—"Statistics of Mines and Mining West of the Rocky Mountains." Rissiter W. Raymon. Page 331.

The "Fish Manuscript—Office of Arizona State Historian.

LOST MINE OF DON MIGUEL PERALTA

Less than an hour's travel from Phoenix, in the foothills of the rugged Superstition Mountains is one of the richest mines ever discovered in the West. This mine is covered over by timber and dirt and all traces of it obliterated. Pieces of rich float are occasionally picked up and stories crop out to prove that the wonderful mine really exists.

The following information was given to the writer by Senor Jose Ballesteros de Madrid at his large cattle ranch in Southern Sonora in 1910. Ballesteros died in the year 1912 at the age of 93 years. His large holdings in Mexico had been bought with Pirate's loot, and Ballesteros passed the rest of his days in comparative security after many years of turbulent adventures.

In the year 1849 Jose Ballesteros de Madrid with two Franciscan priests and fifteen Mexican adventurers sallied forth from the City of Mexico and headed for the California gold fields. This Mexican claims to have located the mine on the Comstock lode in Nevada a few years later, which is still called the Mexican Mine.

After selling his mine for a few thousand dollars, Ballesteros came to the Rio Salado, or Salt River country, and joined a friend by the name of Don Miguel Peralta who was working a fabulously rich mine in the foothills of the rugged Superstition Mountains.

Ballesteros and his men met Don Antonio Pablo Peralta, the father of Miguel, who was on his way to California. Don Antonio told Ballesteros that he and Miguel had been working a mine in the Black Canyon country near what is now Prescott with Doc. Willing, (sometimes called Jack Swilling), Charles Lovejoy, M. Bernalto Gueness, Don Jose Ebarra and Don Rafael Machado.

The ore of this mine having given out the company broke up. Miguel Peralta, with the peons who had worked the mine in Black Canyon, set out to find and work a mine in the Superstition country. Willing, Lovejoy and Gueness stayed at Prescott. Don Antonio Pablo Peralta set out for California with Don Rafael Machado on Oct. 20, 1864, after giving Doc. Willing a deed, on the Black Canyon mine claim sheets, to a floating land grant to a vast acreage of the Territory of Arizona. Being old and feeble Don Antonio Peralta died before he reached any settlement in California and was buried beside the trail. Don Machado died a few years later.

When Senor Jose Ballesteros joined Don Miguel Peralta at his camp on the Rio Salado he took charge of the arrastres where the ore was ground and the

gold recovered by asoga or quicksilver. The camp
and arrastres were located at the bend in the river,
known later as Mormon Flat and now covered by the
waters of Canyon Lake.

Don Miguel took charge of the men at the mines.
Several miners were engaged in getting out the ore
while the rest packed the ore down to the arrastres.
The ore was being taken from an 18-inch vein on
which was a tunnel and shaft. Opposite the tunnel
was a rock house having a sod roof and a porch in
front, in which Don Miguel stayed. The ore from the
vein averaged several thousand dollars to the ton.

Considerable trouble was had with the Indians from
time to time but on account of the great richness of
the ore the Mexicans decided to send for more men
and arms and continue to develop the mine. However,
shortly after this decision had been made and before
more reinforcements could be brought in, the Apaches
raided the mine and after killing all the miners they
ambushed the Requa, or pack train, and all except
three Mexicans, that escaped by hiding in the thick
underbrush, were killed.

When these three men arrived at the river camp
and reported the massacre of all their companions
Ballesteros decided to abandon the mine until it could
be worked with more safety. The camp was immediately abandoned and the small bunch of surviving
adventurers headed for the west coast of Mexico.

After his experience in the roaring mining camps of California and Nevada and with the blood-thirsty Apaches in Arizona, Ballesteros now considered himself a tough hombre from the Rio Salado and shortly thereafter joined a Pirate ship operating near the Isthmus of Panama and engaged in robbing miners and adventurers on their way to and from the California gold fields.

Some of the surviving Mexicans or their relatives evidently returned to work the mine and were discovered by Jacob Walz, the Old Dutchman, and were killed by Walz and his partner, Wiser. Walz found, uncovered the mine, and worked it. When he found that people were following him to try and locate the mine, he again covered the mine with timbers and dirt.

THE LOST DUTCHMAN MINE

For more than half-a-century this mine, whether real or mythical, has held the imagination of the people of Arizona and the Southwest. Its story is one of the most colorful of the West's many mining legends.

And down through the years the hope of finding the valuable mine has steadily faded. Some men have spent the best part of their lives and many thousands of dollars looking for the "Lost Dutchman" mine. Some died while searching, others have been forced to give up because of old age or illness just at the moment when they thought they were on the right trail.

More than 70 years ago, in the '50's, two German prospectors, Jacob Walz and Jacob Wiser, came west to find a fortune. After roaming all over the West, they came, finally, to Arizona. Here the two men worked in the mines, and prospected, eventually locating in Florence, Arizona, and from there prospected the surrounding country.

While prospecting in the Superstition Mountain country they found and worked some placer. Panning being too slow a method the two men returned to Florence, where a carpenter made two dry-washers for them, which they carried to the placer ground. Sometime later, they again returned for supplies, and told the carpenter of finding a rich mine, asking him to go back with them to work it. The carpenter refused, because the Indians were still bad and he was making a good living.

Walz and Wiser worked the mine from then on, at intervals, coming back to Florence for supplies. On arriving back at their camping place, after a trip to Florence for supplies, Walz went out to scout for Indians while Wiser stowed away the supplies. As Walz came up the canyon, in which the mine was located, from the south, he heard pounding and voices. When close enough to see the mine, he discovered two dark-skinned men, dressed only in breechclouts and bandanna headpieces, sitting on the dump. The dark-skinned men were talking and pounding ore in crude rock mortars. Walz thought they were Apaches, so he went back to get Wiser. Sneaking back up the canyon within shooting distance, Walz shot the one on the right, Wiser shooting the one on the left. On close examination they found that the men were Mexicans and not Apaches.

The mine is an old Spanish workings. These two Mexicans knowing the location, had come back to get some gold. Walz and Wiser were sorry they had killed the poor harmless peons, but it was too late to rectify their mistake. The Dutchmen buried the Mexicans and all their possessions close to the mine.

One day in 1881, Walz showed up in Florence without Wiser. When asked about Wiser, he said that Indians had jumped them while he was out hunting and that Wiser had been killed. Due to so many inquiries about his partner, Walz thought the people of Florence suspected him of killing Wiser. Slipping away Walz came to Phoenix where he again became familiar to people of the town. Some few in Phoenix had known him when he was working at the Vulture mine, having been run away from there, because those in charge of the mine suspected him of high-grading.

Jack Walker, of Florence, brother to John D. Walker, told in later years that Wiser had been picked up on the desert, almost dead, by some Pima Indians who brought him to the Walker ranch. Here he died of pneumonia contracted from exposure. Before Wiser died—thinking Walz dead—he gave a map of the mine to Jack Walker with directions telling how to find it. Apparently the Walkers did not look for the mine, having become wealthy from the Vekol mine. The Vekol mine was shown to John D. Walker and P. R. Brady by the Pima Indians. The Walkers were safe among the Pimas, but did not care to risk themselves hunting a mine in Apache country.

In 1882 Walz made a trip to the mine, getting two burro loads of ore which he sold at Tucson to Charlie Myers for $1600. Colonel Poston, George McClarty and Charlie Brown saw the ore and asked questions. Realizing that Walz did not have the mine staked and recorded the three followed the Dutchman to find its location. Walz eluded them in the back country of the Superstitions, after they had followed him to Whitlow's Ranch on Queen Creek.

Walz made his last trip in 1884 and brought back $500 in two little sacks. He was growing feeble, and the trip was extra dangerous for one lone man, so he rented a little house and plot of ground about where Sixteenth Street and Henshaw Road come together, living there until he died in 1892. The old man contracted pneumonia from getting wet while rescuing some of his hogs from the Salt River, which was in flood.

Walz lived partly off of the chickens and hogs that he raised, partly from the revenue of wine made from the grapes of his orchard, and just before he died, partly from the donations of friends. Being German, he liked his beer, and was a constant customer of Luke's Brewery. Walz had many intimate friends, but out of all of these, Rinney Petrarch, and a colored woman, Mrs. Thomas, were the only ones he told about the mine. When under the influence of beer, he liked to spin yarns for anyone who cared to listen.

The Old Dutchman liked Rinney Petrarch particularly, and gave him minute directions of the location of the mine. But Rinney having little interest in the mine paid no attention to the oft-repeated story. After Walz was dead Petrarch could not remember enough of the directions to aid anyone to find the mine. He could only remember the cabin in the cave or under a shelving cliff, a canyon running north and south,

Weaver's Needle
Landmark of the Lost Dutchman

whose floor was full of potholes, a well worn trail leading to the mine, and the old Spanish ranch house where Walz camped over-night.

Rinney's father and his brother, Herman, looked for the mine until the father died. Herman is still looking for and hoping to find it.

Mrs. Thomas, who owned an ice-cream parlor across from the City Hall in Phoenix, sold her place, and being free, set out with Herman Petrarch and his father to look for the mine. The three spent the summer of 1892 in the mountains, but did not find the mine, although they found and identified a trench dug on the Black Queen claim at Goldfield as having been dug by Walz and which was the first mark on the trail to the other mine. Mrs. Thomas is dead now, but she told quite a number of people all that she could remember of the directions to the mine.

The colored woman had taken care of the old German for a number of years, and claimed that he had given her enough gold to buy the fountain for her ice-cream parlor. Mrs. Thomas, according to her story, had dug up a can containing nearly $1500 in gold from the yard, and cashed it at Goldman & Co's. store. She also said that Walz told her to come back for more if that was not enough. Walz could not have had much more for none was found after his death.

This is as much of the secret as one can gather from the different and varied tales: In a gulch in the

130 LOST MINES OF THE GREAT SOUTHWEST

Superstition Mountains, the location of which is beyond a picacho, butte, or sombrero peak is a two-
room house in the mouth of a cave on the side of the
slope near the gulch. The house is located at the foot
of a high bluff, and about a mile and a half from the
mine. The mine is near the head of the gulch and on
the opposite side from the house. The rays of the
setting sun will shine into the tunnel mouth when the
mine is open. The gulch contains many potholes and
runs in a north and south direction.

Near the head of the gulch is the foundation of an
old stone cabin directly opposite the mine. Opposite
the foundation of the cabin is a tunnel, well covered
up and concealed in the bushes. Some distance above
the tunnel, on the side of the mountain, is a shaft or
incline, that is not so steep, but one can climb down.

This too, is concealed carefully and three-quarters
filled with rocks. This shaft goes down on an 18-inch
vein of quartz that will run several thousand dollars
to the ton. This quartz ledge is of the rose-quartz
variety with a few inches of crystal hematite and
quartz on the hanging wall side. The few inches of
the hanging wall ore is about one-third gold. The
rose-quartz is generously sprinkled with pin head size
lumps of gold. Here is a veritable storehouse of the
yellow metal, worth a King's Ransom, waiting for
some lucky fellow.

LOST CEMENT MINE

Related by all the vague troubadors of western America, its legendary history was crystallized by Clemens about 1861.

Somewhere near Mono Lake the marvelous Whiteman Cement Mine was supposed to lie. Every now and then it would be reported that Whiteman had passed through Esmeralda at dead of night, in disguise, and three hours after daylight all the horses and mules and donkeys would be bought, hired or stolen, and half the community would be off for the mountains, following in the wake of Whiteman.

The story is that in the early immigration, about 1841, three young Germans, brothers who had survived an Indian massacre on the plains, wandered on foot through the deserts, avoiding all trails and roads, simply holding a westerly direction and hoping to find California before they starved or died of fatigue. In a gorge in the mountains they sat down to rest, when one of them noticed a curious vein of cement running along the ground, shot full of lumps of dull yellow metal. It was gold, and here was a fortune to be acquired in a single day. The vein was about as wide as a curbstone, and fully two-thirds of it was pure gold. Every pound of the wonderful cement was worth $200. Each brother loaded himself with about twenty-five pounds of it, and they covered up all traces of it, made a rude drawing and started on again.

One of the brothers broke his leg, and was left to die; the second died of thirst, the survivor after incredible hardships was picked up. But after regaining his strength he could not be prevailed upon to abandon his job to join in a search for the vein, although he did draw a detailed map from the first rude drawing and gave it to Whiteman.

Wesley Howell, first mining superintendent of the Copper Queen at Bisbee, Arizona, and Spencer W. Clawson, another mining man of note, are the authorities for the actual existence of such ore as described. The fact that they had seen and handled the rich "cement" ore must be accepted as proof that there was something back of the tale of the Lost Cement Mine.

THE LOST SHOEMAKER PLACER

Charles A. Roderic, an old-time prospector, who was for some years engaged in the shoemaker's trade in Phoenix, Arizona, was prospecting with two other men in the Four Peaks country in 1877. Although the Indians were hostile they managed to push into a rough and undeveloped country, never before entered by white men. The three men found gold in great quantities in ledges as well as placer.

Roderic obtained $73.50 from one shovelful of the placer, which he kept for a number of years to show to skeptics.

The three men stayed in the secluded place only long enough to build a sluice box, and shovel up a quantity of dirt to put through it. A war party of Tonto Apaches jumped them and the three were forced to flee to save their lives. So hurriedly had they worked and then fled that their sense of the location of the place was none too good. However, after reaching Phoenix they prepared to go back.

Ill luck descended upon them once more, for as they were crossing a bridge on the Grand Canal one of their burros shied, knocking one of the men into the canal along with another burro and the supplies from the backs of the two burros. The partner who fell in was drowned before Roderic and the other man could rescue him. The two survivors turned back to Phoenix.

The other partner went to California, but before going made Roderic agree not to look for the mine until he came back to join him. Several years later, about 1890, he died leaving Roderic the sole possessor of the secret.

Roderic having saved some money decided to go search for the mine. On his way to the mine he suffered sunstroke while crossing the desert and lay for five days before found and rescued. But back in Phoenix the hungry wolf haunted himself and family as well as sickness and he was unable to look for the mine until 1892. His efforts were unsuccessful then or later, although he looked for it for many years before he died. Many prominent men in Phoenix grubstaked him often.

The main reason he did not find the mine was because he searched practically the same stretch of country every time he went out.

If you find a shovel, and pick sticking in a pile of dirt, an old hand-hewn sluice box, beside a small stream lined with cottonwoods in the Four Peaks country, you can rest assured that you have located The Lost Shoemaker Placer. Old Man Depression will bother you no longer, for ground that yields $73.50 to the first shovel full must be rich.

MONTEZUMA'S TREASURE

It was in the beautiful little mining town of Ajo, Pima County, Arizona, that I first heard the story of Montezuma's Treasure. Hidden away for more than four centuries in the secret recesses of the barren and fantastic Ajo Mountains below Montezuma's Head is a great treasure of such wonderful richness that it was guarded night and day for three hundred years, and to this day no Indian will disclose its location. There is no ancient chart so essential in fiction to aid the search for this treasure; only the word of mouth handed down from father to son. There is a tradition among the Papago Indians that their ancestors helped bury the treasure in the mountain cave beneath Montezuma's Head and that it is guarded by no other than Montezuma himself.

For a hundred miles in every direction from the Ajo Mountains this lofty peak resembling the head and shoulders of a large Indian can be seen clearly outlined against the sky as he sits majestically on top of the mountain. This great store of gold running into millions of dollars in value was taken from the placer mines in Mexico a short distance to the south. These ancient mines were of such great richness that many tons of pure gold was picked up from the surface of the ground and the creek beds where it had been collected by erosion. The Indians say that after the treasure had been safely stored away in the cave Montezuma climbed up to the mountain top and turned to stone. Today this arrogant stone god sits on his mountain throne overlooking the peaceful valleys and boundless plains that once teemed with animal life and prehistoric man. The ancient dwellings near the base of the mountain have long since fallen into decay. Their rooms are deserted now and the happy voices of the Indians have passed into silence. The sound of music and moccasined feet have likewise passed on. Corn grinders and pieces of broken pottery and some ancient graves is all that is left to remind us of the red men that once prospered here.

The Ajo Mountains is the home of the storm gods and in the rainy season dark clouds hang over Montezuma's Head, flashes of lightning chase each other up the ridges, and thunder rumbles through the canyon walls and torrents of rain descend from the mountain sides into the valley below.

On these stormy days Papago Indians in the nearby villages sit around the camp fires and in hushed tones talk about the great treasure stored away in the mountain cave. They believe that some day the spirit of Montezuma will come out of the East and then he will climb down from the mountain top and open the secret cave and then all the wealth that it contains will be given to the Indians to whom it rightfully belongs.

When the Spanish conquerored Mexico in 1521, the
Aztecs buried their great treasures to keep them from
falling into the hands of their greedy conquerors,
and most of them have remained buried ever since.
Of the many thousands of people that pass over the
highway between Tucson and Ajo every year, few of
them have ever heard of the fabulous treasure stored
away in the sombre mountain beneath Montezuma's
Head.   Those who would search for the treasure as
many have done before, should bear in mind the story
of the old Papagoes handed down from father to son,
"When the Indians were engaged in storing the gold
away in the cave they were so close that they could
on a still night, hear the tom-toms beat and the dogs
bark in the village below."

138 LOST MINES OF THE GREAT SOUTHWEST

LOST MINE OF SAN ANTONE

A rich mine was said to have been located in the eastern part of New Mexico in 1660, but was abandoned in course of time, owing to hostility of Indians. The old Spanish custom of enslaving the Indians and forcing them to work in the mines was still being carried out at this time. The Indians, of course, resented the practice mightily.

From records of the amount of Tithes paid to the Catholic Church, it is estimated that this mine produced about $60,000,000 in gold.

San Antone set out in 1800 to find the mine and actually found it in 1804. Not being prepared to work it, he and his followers got together what gold they could carry and set out for a Mission on the coast where they could get assistance. To guide them back to the mine they drove stakes on the plains, but San Antone fell sick at the place where the city of San Antonio now stands and died there. Indians and desperadoes murdered his companions for their gold. Only one member of the expedition lived to tell the tale. The stakes they had set out, not being cared for, soon fell away and the mine was lost once again.

There are no maps left to guide seekers of the lost mine, and the information obtainable is only meagre.

SHEPHERD'S LOST MINE

An old trunk bought as "old junk" at a sale of unclaimed railroad freight uncovered the story of a lost mine near Tucson, Arizona. Frank Brubaker, of Omaha, Nebraska, bought the trunk, which had been on hand so long the railroad was unable to trace its origin. In the trunk was a bag of mud and a lot of old papers.

Brubaker took the mud to the smelter, but threw away the old papers. The mud proved to be gold, worth $1,845, which the smelter refused to return to Brubaker, contending that the real owner might claim the payment. Brubaker resorted to the courts.

Frank Kelly, a bricklayer of Omaha, Nebraska, appeared to claim the trunk and contents for his wife. Kelly's wife had been searching for the trunk, not for the gold, but for a map to a lost mine contained in the trunk.

Mrs. Kelly was formerly Mrs. De Estine Shepherd, of Quincy, Illinois, where she ran a boarding house.

De Estine Shepherd came to her house in November, 1905, to room. He was ill, but had money—gold. Shepherd told Mrs. Kelly that he was a miner and had been searching for his brother, of whom he had lost trace.

Shepherd grew worse and was on the point of death. After the physicians had given him up, he told the landlady about his mine in Arizona and gave her a rough sketch of its location. Also that there was a trunk in a boarding house kept by Mrs. Almina Hicks in Tucson, Arizona, which contained a bag of gold, a quart whiskey bottle full of gold, a detailed map of the location of the mine, and some papers.

"Marry me, be my widow, and inherit it all," urged the dying man of Mrs. Kelly. "You have been good to me and I have no one to leave the property to."

The landlady held out a couple of days, but finally gave in. The marriage took place in St. Mary's Hospital, where Shepherd was, on December 29, 1905. Shepherd died the next day, and was buried in Graceland Cemetery, Quincy.

Mrs. Shepherd and a lawyer, with the money the gold miner left her, came to Tucson. She had a rough map drawn by Shepherd upon his death-bed, as well as papers showing she was the widow and heir of the miner.

At Tucson they could not locate the missing trunk with the bag of gold and the map. Mrs. Almina Hicks had given up her boarding house and had gone to Mexico.

Shepherd, they found, was well known in Tucson. He had prospected around there for thirty years or so. He would come into Tucson, load up his pack horse with supplies and go back to the mountains. He always paid for his supplies with gold dust.

Shepherd on his deathbed told his wife that he had located this mine and had worked it for twenty-three years. The mine was extremely rich, but he had only taken out enough gold to keep him going. The balance he had cached within the mine itself.

"There is $5,000,000 worth of gold in that cache," he told her. "And the mine itself is full of gold."

Mrs. Shepherd, the lawyer, and a guide tried to find the mine from the rough map the miner had drawn before his death, but were not successful. They worked around the location, which Shepherd said was fifty-five miles south of Tucson, for six months. They also tried to locate Mrs. Hicks, but were unsuccessful there also.

Later Mrs. Shepherd married Mr. Kelly and moved to Omaha.

The above story appeared in a Los Angeles paper in 1924 and recalled a former experience that M. F. Rose had with the mine in 1920.

Rose, making a trip from North Carolina to Palo Alto, California, by train, struck up an acquaintance with an elderly gentleman, whose name he has forgotten. The elderly gentleman was a graduate of an Eastern mining school; Rose was coming west to begin a course of mining at Stanford University. Having a common ground on which to meet the two became friendly, the elderly man telling the younger about a mine that he was working, and had worked for 15 years or more. This mine was located fifty-five miles south of Tucson.

At Tucson the gentleman was to meet an old prospector with some burros and go direct to the mine. When the train pulled up at the old wooden station at sunrise Rose was on hand to watch the departure of his acquaintance.

The porter handed down his baggage which an old prospector came forward to get and load on two burros standing a few feet away. The elderly gentleman pulled his hat down over his eyes, got off of the train, went forward to get a dog from the express car. On coming back he greeted the old prospector, waved goodbye to Rose, then started out with the man, the two burros, and the dog. Before getting off the train he had promised to meet Rose on the return trip and show him the ore.

Sure enough, when the train on which Rose was returning east, arrived in Tucson, the old prospector was standing beside two burros and a bunch of suit-cases. The old prospector and the porter lifted the suit-cases, which were quite heavy, on to the train. The prospector and the burros turned about, disappearing down an alley. A few minutes later the elderly gentleman, with his hat pulled down over his eyes, appeared from the alley. He boarded the train, going immediately to the smoker where Rose met him.

After the train was on its way he took Rose to his berth, and opened up one of the suit-cases. There were three good sized suit-cases, especially made for the purpose. Inside the suit-cases was a white quartz rock containing, he said, 75 per cent gold. The gold was in large angular chunks, some of the nuggets being as large as the little finger.

Each of the three suit-cases had around $12,000 worth of the rock. He also had a sample sack, which he carried in his hand that was all pure gold, which had been separated from the rock. This represented his half of the total amount of rock the two had worked out. The old prospector was returning to the mine to get his share.

The elderly gentleman had met the prospector in Canada. The prospector knowing of the rich mine near Tucson, told the Engineer about it. The Engineer grubstaked him to find and work it, which he did. The prospector worked the mine, the Engineer only coming out once in awhile to get and take his share back east.

"This is our last trip to the mine," said the old gentleman. "The old prospector is going to get his share, cover up the mine, and is then going to Canada to spend the rest of his days. There is still plenty of gold left in the mine, so, if you need money sometime, come to Tucson, go south for fifty-five miles, then west for two miles. The mine is in a gulch that drains south. It is all yours if you want it."

Rose has never looked for the mine, but may later. However, he is passing on the information for any one who wishes to do so. This mine is so rich that alongside of it, other lost mines are what a Scotchman would toss into a blind man's hat.

PEN-HACH-A-PE MINE OR THE "LOST FRENCHMAN"

Some years ago, about 1869, two Frenchmen came to Yuma with a large quantity of gold which had been hammered out of quartz. Sight of the gold caused great excitement as all know that gold obtained that way must be from a very rich vein.

After buying their supplies from W. B. Hooper & Co's. store in Yuma the two men still had $8,000 left on deposit at the store. The money was still on deposit at the store as late as 1889 which was twenty years after the two Frenchmen had deposited it there. The store was later known as Hooper, Barney & Co. and is now out of business.

These two men are supposed to be the original discoverers of the Penhachape Mine.

When the two Frenchmen left town after getting supplies they went in the direction of the Eagle Tail Mountains. Half the population of Yuma followed, but the Frenchmen eluded the pursuit at night. That was the last seen or heard of them.

Some time later two skeletons were found in the mountains which some supposed was all that remained of the Frenchmen. They had, probably, been killed by the Apaches who were concentrated in large numbers in that vicinity.

Piles of rich ore had been discovered about 1873 by King Woolsey while on one of his scalp hunting forages after Indians. The ore was stacked up beside a well defined trail. Due to the unsettled state of the country the ore lay there for several more years until Woolsey could organize an expedition to come after the ore and to find the mine. Woolsey and his band dared not stop very long in one place or burden themselves with anything but scalps, food, and ammunition as the Apaches hunted Woolsey as much as he hunted the Apaches. Many lives in Arizona would have been saved if the Apaches had been able to capture the Woolsey band, and deal out a just death to them.

A later expedition found and removed the ore, but could not locate the mine. The name Penhachape came from the name of the pass in which the ore was stacked. Many have looked for the Penhachape Mine since the story of the ore became public.

In 1889 Mr. Lincoln Fowler and his brother while prospecting near the Bonanza Mine in the Harqua Hala District discovered a large excavation on a ledge which they were tracing up. Careful examination of the hole showed that pick and drill had been at work there, but every vestige of the ore had been removed except a few loose pieces on the ground.

The camp of the original locators was found. Near it was a mesquite tree with the limbs trimmed off except one limb which pointed up towards the ledge at the exact point of the opening. The bleached bones of the skeleton of a man was also found close by the camp. The work and camp was undoubtedly white man's work and the skull of the skeleton looked more like a white man's than an Indian's.

Mr. A. H. Peeples mentions three Frenchmen who were camped in that vicinity just prior to 1868. These men were mining, and were doing fairly well until they had trouble with the Indians nearby who were Maricopas. Peeples passed the camp of the Frenchmen and Indians on an expedition, heading northeast from Yuma, on unknown business. On the return trip to Yuma Peeples found the cabin that the Frenchmen were using burned and some dead Indians nearby. Later he heard that a drunken brawl had taken place there and the Indians had run the three white men off, but not without casualties. From the description of the two men who came to Yuma, he identified two of them. The bleached skeleton at the mine probably was all that remained of the third. The Maricopas may have been the ones who killed all three men.

There will be those who will not agree that the Penhachape Mine and the Lost Frenchman are the same, but the facts above are well authenticated, yet the Lost Frenchman may still be waiting in the Eagle Tails for some lucky man to find.

LOST DUTCH OVEN MINE

Somewhere in the Clipper Mountains in Southern California is a fabulously rich mine. The lucky finder, truly, will have reached the golden staircase to luxury and ease. The old Dutch Oven alone will furnish enough gold, in grains, dust, flakes, and chunks to support a man comfortably for several years.

A mining man, Thomas Scofield, of Los Angeles, found and brought back some fabulously rich ore from the Clipper Mountains. In 1894 Scofield was drilling a tunnel, to tap underground water, in the Clipper Mountains, north of Danby, California, for the Santa Fe Railroad.

Danby is located on Highway 66, a paved road across Southern California. The road runs from Needles to Barstow, over the Cajon Pass to San Bernardino, thence to Los Angeles. Danby itself is comprised of a water tank, a section house, and a filling station.

Scofield, having nothing better to do on his days off, prospected the unnamed canyons and draws of the Clipper Mountains. One day in June, he wandered into a gulch or draw that contained a fair-sized spring. A narrow trail leading up the canyon from the water hole.

Scofield's curiosity was aroused, as he knew of no one living or prospecting in that country. According to mining men, the Clipper Mountains are not the right kind of place for the finding of gold.

Setting out to follow the trail, Scofield crossed over two ridges to some small hills, and into another canyon.

Coming to a blank wall, he retraced his steps to where the trail wound up the steep side of a hill. Moving up this trail he passed between two huge upright rocks. The passage way between the rocks was barely wide enough to allow a packed animal through. Beyond these two rocks stood another huge boulder; a dark black in color.

Turning the corner of the boulder he saw a tent pole with torn shreds of canvas flapping in the wind. Below the pole was a bed of dried boughs covered by a threadbare blanket. Nearby was a pile of railroad ties, some being split into wedges and lagging for timbering a mine. Some short lengths of drill steel, a heavy hammer, rusty axes, picks, and shovels lay scattered about.

The camp had been long deserted. There were no clues to tell of the owner or what had become of him. Looking about Scofield saw a large Dutch Oven off to one side of the camp. The trail leading on past the camp he followed for a short distance to a shaft.

The shaft had been sunk on a series of parallel stringers or veins. The veins were in a bluish quartz formation and were almost solid gold. They could be traced for some distance, and seemed to widen instead of pinching out. So fascinated by his find, he failed to notice that the sun was fast going down.

The sun slipped behind the far hills. Scofield, though cold and hungry, lay down to sleep in the ghostly treasure camp.

Scofield was up with the dawn. The shaft on which considerable work had been done engaged his attention. The old windlass with rope and bucket attached was still strong enough to use. Dropping the bucket down slowly he estimated the depth of the shaft as being between seventy and eighty feet. None of the ore had been shipped as the pile of ore on the dump was of the right amount for the depth of the shaft.

Picking a few prize specimens of rock Scofield went back to the deserted camp. As he started to leave the Old Dutch Oven caught his eye. Kicking the lid off he was surprised to find it more than half full of virgin gold. Filling his pockets with the precious stuff he hurried on as he was very hungry and thirsty, camp food being a long way off.

As he journeyed back down the trail, his mind full of day dreams, Scofield forgot to look back and fix landmarks in his mind. He followed the trail mechanically, not even noticing his direction of travel.

He did not stop at Danby but continued on to Los Angeles. Once he arrived there he had the samples assayed. The results were so good that the assayer would not believe that the dump was composed of rock that even ran half that high.

Scofield realized nearly a thousand dollars from the gold in his pockets plus that in the samples. Feeling rich and wishing a few days rest he stayed a few weeks in town.

Finally he found a partner to his liking and they set out to find the mine. But after a few days searching with no results, the partner became disgusted.

Scofield was never able to find the trail or has any one else. The old ghost camp with the Old Dutch Oven full of gold, and a larger supply of the same gold that remains to be mined is still out there in the Clipper Mountains just as Scofield left them.

If you decide to look for this fabulous wealth go to Danby prepared for a long stay, for the mountains will have to be combed to find this mine.

WESTWARD BOUND

When gold was discovered in California in 1849, and hardy pioneers were crowding the Santa Fe Trail on their way to the new El Dorado, a wagon train composed of fourteen prairie schooners hauled by oxen, left San Antonio, Texas, for California. The Texas plains were swarming with hostile Indians and in order to travel with more safety, a large number of families journeyed from their old homes to San Antonio to join the wagon train that was soon to start on the long journey across the plains to the new gold fields. Fourteen families with a large number of men, women and children made up the company. The men were all well armed and besides household goods and other supplies to be used in furnishing their new homes in the west, they carried $50,000 in gold.

After having many narrow escapes from being killed by the hostile Indians on the great plains, the little party reached El Paso where they camped for several days to rest the cattle and themselves. Here one family dropped out and returned to their former home, making the trip back with freighters that were crossing the plains from El Paso to San Antonio. Of this family we will have more to say later. Each night when camp was made the wagons were thrown into a circle to afford more protection against the Indians and prevent the stock from being run off during the night. The $50,000 belonging to the company was carried in an iron chest and for safe keeping was buried each night within the circle made by the wagons. After resting at El Paso the party headed west making for a crossing on the Gila River. After striking the Gila they passed through the friendly Pima villages purchasing corn, beans, wheat and many kinds of vegetables grown by the Pimas. Crossing a branch of the Gila near the present Saint Catherine Mission, they headed south around the point of the Estrella Mountains and when in the vicinity of the peak known as Montezuma's Head, they camped for the night. As usual the wagons were formed into a circle as had been the custom since leaving Texas and the iron chest was then buried somewhere within the circle.

About daybreak the next morning a large band of Apache Indians on their way to the north from the gulf, swooped down upon them from the surrounding hills. The Texans put up a valiant fight but being taken by surprise and greatly outnumbered they were all killed. The wagons were burned and the cattle driven off. Word of the terrible tragedy soon reached Texas and the friends that had saved their lives by returning from El Paso, told the story of how the iron chest was buried each night within the circle made by the wagons. Pieces of burned iron can still be seen on the desert below the mountain peak. No systematic effort has ever been made to recover the treasure. Many years ago a telegraph operator at Maricopa, while prospecting or riding over the country around the south end of the Estrella Mountains found an old post with some peculiar markings on it. Returning to Maricopa he reported that he had found the spot where the treasure had been cached by the Texans. Getting a leave of absence from duty for several days he returned to the Estrellas and began operations. After he had dug up an acre or two of ground around the post without finding any gold, some one happened along that way and informed him that the post around which he had been digging was a Government Survey post marking a corner of the Pima Indian Reservation. In so far as I know no one else has ever tried to find the old chest and the $50,-000 in gold.

THE LOST BLUE BUCKET PLACER

During the year 1845, four years before the California gold rush, an emigrant train was crossing plain, desert and mountains. Oregon was the goal or El Dorado sought by the men, women, and children who comprised this train. Gold was not the guiding star, but land. Yes, acres and acres of rich, well-watered timber lands.

The band of emigrants worked their way across country by aid of a compass. They crossed plain, desert, and mountains keeping on a straight course. If a large mountain stood in their way, they crossed instead of going around.

Finally the band reached what is now the famous Gravelly Ford Crossing on the Humboldt River. Here they split in two parties. One party continued along the Humboldt, the other group striking their way due north by the Black Rock Mountains. From the latter party a strange tale originated years afterwards.

After leaving the Black Rock Mountains behind them they came to a high mountain range. The slopes toward which the train was headed were gradual and the party managed to get to the top with the wagons.

Upon reaching the top the Chief of the Train could get a good view of the surrounding country and took bearings on the Twin Sister Peaks. The western side of the mountains being very steep the party cut timbers to drag behind the wagons for braking power.

In those days people used lock chains on the wheel of the wagon for brakes. The descent being too steep for this method of braking, timbers were cut and chained to the wagons. The timbers were allowed to drag perpendicular to the wagon. They were then let down the grade.

While the wagons were being let down, camp was made on a spring in the canyon. Some of the members of the outfit picked up chunks of what looked to them like brass.

These people did not know that gold could be found that way. They were only farmers, and probably knew very little about gold in any form.

The children picked up quite a few of the yellow stones to play with. Several buckets being filled with the pretty rocks. The buckets that hung beneath the wagons were painted the same color as the wagons—blue.

While camped at the spring one of the women became sick and died. They buried her near the spring, heaping up rocks upon the grave, and leaving one of the blue buckets hanging above on a bush.

After successfully crossing the mountains the party continued the journey, unaware of the fortune in gold swinging in the blue buckets beneath the wagons. The emigrants had more grief while crossing the Deschutes River. The wagons capsized, the buckets were lost or spilled their contents out. Only a few of the yellow stones were saved. These the children were playing with in the wagons or carrying in their pockets.

The party reaching Northwestern Oregon, settled on homesteads, and commenced the arduous task of living in wild, untrammeled west. Several years later some few of these settlers moved down to Sutter's Fort in California. Here they saw the nuggets recovered by Marshall at the mill site. The nuggets looked just like the yellow stones picked up by them in eastern Oregon. Obtaining some of the nuggets from the settlers in Oregon, they showed them around. The bright stones were pure gold.

So much excitement was created that a party of ninety persons was organized to find the rich mine, already known as the Blue Bucket Placer.

Hostile Indians soon put a damper on the party. The outfit was ambushed, more than half the members being killed. Only two men who knew, or thought they knew, the location of the golden canyon survived to get back to California. These two were members of the original emigrant party. These two died shortly afterwards due to the hardships suffered. They met and told a Dr. Drane, of Yreka, the story and gave him specific instructions how to find the canyon before dying.

Dr. Drane was quite content with his bird in hand. He was running a store and hotel, placering on the side. Doing fairly well, he was loath to leave and hunt for the two birds in the bush. But the golden birds were doomed to multiply.

A trapper, of the Hudson Bay variety, stopped at Yreka on his way south to the gold fields. The doctor showed him some of the gold that he daily washed out in his long tom sluice box.

"If that is gold," said the trapper, "I know where there is a pile of them little stones."

"In a steep walled canyon north and east from here are lots of them. Some bigger and some smaller. A man could load two horses with all they could carry in half a day. Why you could just pick them up out of the stream bed."

The trapper, it seems, had wintered his horses in the canyon, finding the gold there the following spring when he retrieved the animals

Describing the place minutely, something clicked in Dr. Dane's head. He recalled the story of the two sick men. Yes, assuredly, the two places were one and the same. The interest of the doctor grew and grew.

The doctor, the trapper, and a friend of the doctor set out. The trapper back-tracking himself by the dead embers of his campfires. Not until they reached the head of Goose Lake Valley, did the doctor know where he was and where he was going. From the top of Warner Hill the doctor could see the surrounding country, and finally got his bearings.

The trapper pointed out two peaks to the north and east about 120 miles away. "Thar," said the trapper, "That mountain off to the right is the one. The canyon lays on this side and to the north of it. That is where I put my animals out to graze. The creek runs big in spring, small in the fall. The canyon's level at the lower end. There's a trail into it, and lots of grass. The upper end is steep as all-get-out. The walls are so steep it's about all a man can do to get a horse through."

The three found the place as described, but were doomed to disappointment. A recent cloudburst had played havoc with the canyon. The stream bed was piled high with brush, boulders, and sand.

The trio looked long and hard, but not a trace of gold could they find. The doctor never doubted that they were in the right place, but then he may have been wrong. With their food supply almost gone, and being exhausted from their search, they gave up the quest, reluctantly.

Some twenty or more years later, in 1879, a boy, G. S. Johnston, and a man, William Adams, were traveling across Oregon. From Malhuer Lakes they headed into and camped at the Agency of the Malheur Indian Reservation. Adams, an old California miner, liked the looks of the rocks and formations of the country in and around the old agency buildings.

The Malheur Reservation at that time was located where Harney, Grant, and Malheur Counties join. The Agency was located on the southwestern slopes of the Burnt River Mountains, west of Beulah, and north of Drewsey. White men were not allowed to stay very long on the Reservation, or to prospect for minerals at that time.

Mr. Johnston remembered a conversation with the agent while camped here. The agent had found piles of old rotted timbers, a grave by a spring, and a wide deep track down the mountain, about three miles from the Agency. The timbers had been used behind wagons for brakes, and had cut a large swath or road down the mountain. Over 50 years later he hears the story of the Blue Bucket Placer and recalls the tale told by the Agent.

The story of Mr. Johnston should give new hope to seekers of the Lost Blue Bucket Placer. It may be that the old trapper led Dr. Dane to the wrong canyon, or perhaps the elements of nature have now washed the excess debris of the canyon away. The golden horde may now be within the reach of some lucky, hard-working, prospector. The prize is well worth a search of the district now so definitely located by the memory of an almost forgotten event.

LOST MINE OF THE LITTLE BROWN MEN

In the Northwestern part of Nevada, according to recorded accounts, there is a rich mine. Nuggets big as hen's eggs have been picked up there. This mine which has been known for a long time received the name, Lost Mine of the Little Brown Men, because Indians brought gold from it to trade for the goods of the white man.

Job Taylor, an Indian trader who lived and did a very fine business in Indian Valley, first saw the nuggets. Indians with gold dust were numerous and did not excite anyone, much less the matter of fact, Taylor. He attended to his own business paying little heed to the idle gossip coming across the counter. In fact he paid little attention to what anybody might have to say about anything.

So, one day, when an Indian appeared, unrolled his blanket and disclosed a large hunk of pure gold. Taylor didn't get excited. He did try by all known means to get the Indian to tell him where it came from, without success.

Being the kind of man he was, Job promptly forgot about the Indian and his gold. Yes, he was truly a hard man to excite.

The following year the Indian once more appeared with a bunch of the same gold rocks. This time when coaxing, cajolery, and promises failed to elicit the desired information, he tried threats. But once more the Indian left without revealing the secret. When he did come back the third time, Taylor was almost frantic. Only after he offered the Indian practically everything in the trading post, did the Indian agree to show him from whence the nuggets came.

Job in company of old Captain Wetherall, a noted Indian fighter, set out from Indian Valley with the Little Brown man. They went down to Susanville, California, and kept on the Honey Lake Road. They camped by the spring at Deep Hole, Nevada.

"Two sleeps," said the Indian, "Catchum gold."

At Deep Hole, the guide left to carry a message to Chief Winnemuca, of the Paiutes. He promised to come right back.

In the morning the Indian came back, but he was a changed man. No amount of persuasion could induce him to continue the search.

Gold-seeking whites ruined good Indian country according to the guide. Winnemuca said that it would be dangerous for them to continue. The guide, especially, had probably been threatened with dire punishment.

Turning back, Job and Wetherall went back to Indian Valley. Taylor continued trading, charging off the trip to experience. Then came a small Indian lad with some of the same golden nuggets. This was too much. The joke had gone too far.

From the Indian boy, by bribery and threats, Job learned that the older Indians found the gold in a steep, rock-strewn canyon. He was willing to direct Taylor only he did not know where it was. The boy told of an old Indian who was in disfavor of the tribe, but who knew the location and would probably tell its location.

Setting out on the same path as before they finally came to Deep Hole and camped. They found the old Indian, but could not induce him to part with the secret.

There was nothing left for the two men to do but get the lad to guide them for he must have heard where the canyon was located. The boy, thoroughly scared of the two men and what they might do to him, consented to guide them on. They started off in the same direction pointed out by the other Indian.

At the first camp made after leaving Deep Hole Captain Wetherall remarked that he would kill that blinkety-blanked Indian if he did not find the mine. The boy must have heard the remark for next morning he was gone. That idle remark probably cost them the mine.

The search for the mine still goes on. Some think that the mine lies in a canyon one and a half miles east from Eblings in Virgin Valley, Humboldt County, Nevada. The secret has been carried to the grave with the Little Brown Men who gathered the golden rocks to trade for the gaudy, cheap goods of the white man. Mayhap, there are some left who know of the location and will tell the secret to some honest prospector who will not cheat them of their share.

LOST COWBOY MINE

In the early sixties about the time La Paz and Rich Hill were booming and millions in gold dust and nuggets were being taken out of the gulches, cowboys riding over the brush and cactus-covered desert down on the Colorado River somewhere to the north of Yuma, were throwing black gold nuggets at long-horned cattle in order to chase them into an adobe corral. This corral was built on the edge of the desert near the foot of a small round hill. This hill was covered with gravel and water-worn pebbles composed of chunks of brown or black hematite which showed free gold when broken open. There were other chunks of a black heavy metal scattered among the chunks of iron.

Just how long the ranch was in operation or who it belonged to is unknown, but about 50 years later it was discovered that the black nuggets were tarnished gold. One of the cowboys had gone east after the ranch had been raided by Apache Indians and a number of employes killed and the cattle and horses driven off. The cowboy had several pieces of the gold in an old trunk that he had taken east with him upon leaving the ranch many years before. He showed these pieces of heavy metal to a mining man who pronounced them to be tarnished gold nuggets and of great value. Ever since that date the search for the adobe corral has been going on. Many prospectors and desert rats have, no doubt, camped at the corral and could return to it if they knew of the great amount of gold scattered around it.

A cowboy in the days of the California gold rush, showed up at Mojave, California, many years ago with his saddle bags full of black gold nuggets and reported that he had found them on or near a small round hill in the direction of the Colorado River. It is now believed by many that the cowboy either found the corral across on the east side of the Colorado River in Arizona, or that he got his gold from the body of a dead Indian that had reached the great deposit of black gold located somewhere in the great desert east of Indio, California, and had died from thirst and the intense heat on the way out.

The cowboy told the mining man that the black nuggets covered several acres of ground around the corral at the foot of the little hill. A prospector well known in Yuma, camped at the corral one night and many years later hearing of the gold there tried to return to it but was found dead on the desert several weeks later with an empty canteen by his side. The mining man returned to the west and tried to locate the adobe corral, but was never able to find any trace of it. The search has been going on ever since.

Aviators flying over that part of the desert have reported seeing an old corral that answers the description. Other men will brave the desert heat as many have done before to search for this legendary mine and no doubt a million dollars worth of gold could be picked up from the ground around this adobe corral described by the old cowboy.

GERONIMO'S MINE

While Geronimo was in prison at Fort Sill, Oklahoma, he tried to bribe an officer of the Army to set him free. The reward held out was a rich mine in the haunts of the Apache Indians. He did not give enough information for the officer to go look for the mine himself. The officer was to go along, and Geronimo was to show him the mine. The plot was discovered and the officer court-martialed. The Old Indian Chieftain was kept more closely confined.

Will James, interpreter at Fort Sill, and a friend of Geronimo, said that the mine was in the Verde River country, Arizona, and furnished the material from which the Indians made their green beads.

James also told a story of a gold mine one mile southeast of the Bead Mine. The gold mine being in a deep box canyon to which there were only three entrances. These means of ingress were very difficult to negotiate. It is so difficult in fact that ropes or ladders would have to be used.

On the floor of the canyon is a spring near an old stone, or adobe house. The house has been crushed down by a large boulder rolled into the canyon by Indians to kill workers of the mine. This is the mine from which the Redmen took large gold nuggets that were cashed in Tempe.

Some think the mine is located on the old Reservation assigned to Geronimo and his band near Winkelman, Arizona.

SILVER MOUNTAIN

During the early '90's a party of Mexicans from Sonora, headed by Pedro Encinas, stopped at the San Carlos Indian Agency on their way in search of what was described as a Mountain of Silver. This mountain, it was said, was in the vicinity, but whether within or without the limits of the Reservation the searchers were uncertain.

Many years before a veritable Mountain of Silver had been discovered by a Mexican relative of Encinas. This relative described the ground in the most glowing of terms. Big and little black nuggets of native silver cover the ground. There is also, red, green, and black silver in the large veins which cut the mountain. The veins are more than half silver. Truly, it is a Mountain of Silver.

Great age and increasing infirmities had prevented the relative of Encinas from returning for the treasure. Dying, the old man bequeathed his secret to his descendants. Of these, Pedro was the only one familiar with the country and gathering about him a party of friends and relatives for greater strength, told them of the quest and offered to guide them to the Silver Mountain.

With letters of recommendation from the Governor of Sonora, the party started its pack train north and in due time came to San Carlos, delivering the letters to W. J. Ellis, Acting Indian Agent.

The adventurers were well received and permission was given them to search—provided that should the Silver Mountain be found on the Reservation, exploration should cease and the expedition return.

L. K. Thompson, of Salt River, who is a brother-in-law of Encinas, accompanied the party, which, after several days travel came, at last, to a mountain which the guide, from the description that had been given him, pronounced to be the object of their search. It lay, however, within the Reservation, and agreeable to their pledge, they turned about to abandon the treasure.

On their way out they came upon evidence that others, whose presence in the country had been very recent, had not been so scrupulous, for there were monuments marking claims, workings, and camps.

Still on their way out they encamped by a stream, and here found the traces of a frightful tragedy—the work, doubtless, of Apache Indians. Upon the yielding earth were the impressions of the bodies of several campers who had gone to sleep there in fancied security. Cooking utensils were scattered all about, battered as if to purposely destroy their usefulness and there were found also a pick, a shovel, three cartridge belts and some tattered remnants of clothing.

Close down by the bed of the stream were the dead embers of a great fire, and in the ashes there were partly burned human bones, a sack of corn and the charred remnants of three saddles. Near by was a canteen, partially filled with water that was fresh. There was no ore about.

This was all that was left of a party that had evidently found the Silver Mountain.

The Encinas party returned to Mexico without telling the exact whereabouts of the mine to a single soul. L. K. Thompson of Salt River Valley was then the only one in Arizona who knew of the location of the mine. That is why the Silver Mountain joined the host of other lost mines.

FINIS.

NOTES

The Stories contained in this Book adhere as closely to the true facts as is possible. Each and every story has been verified and authenticated. The tracing down and weeding out process has taken a great deal of time and energy. Many will disagree with the data contained herein, but that is as it should be. Many lost mines could have been found and made to yield up their treasure if those who had information, or think they had, could have agreed instead of disagreed.

Many men hold on tight to any little knowledge of lost mines that they have despite the fact that they have repeatedly failed to find the mines through such information. All information, if lumped together, might prove valuable. The data and stories here have been compiled from a wealth of information, but it is possible that some still hold the missing clue.

The Author is indebted to Milton F. Rose, of Mesa, Arizona, for verifications and contributions to the following stories: The Doctor Thorne Mine, The Lost Yuma Mine, Lost Squaw Hollow Mine, Lost Adam's Diggings, The Miner Expedition, The Lost Dutchman Mine, Lost Shoemaker Placer, Shepherd's Lost Mine, Lost Blue Bucket Mine, Mine of Don Miguel Peralta.

NOTES—Continued

THE LOST TAYOPE MINE:

General George Crook and his soldiers while trying to capture Geronimo and his band passed by the old Tayope Mine. A few others have also passed the old mine, but have been unable to relocate it. The country is unbelievably rough, and it is possible to pass within a short distance of the old buildings and yet not see them.

Legend has it, that the bells of the church could be heard in Nacori which is over sixty miles from the mine. The mine being located in or near the Canyon of the Caves. This canyon is in the heart of Geronimo's stronghold in Mexico. There are still many wild Apaches, descendants of the old Chief's band, living in the stronghold today.

THE MINE OF DON MIGUEL PERALTA OR THE LOST DUTCHMAN:

Don Miguel Peralta had no children, and was probably killed by Indians. Ballesteros did not say he was killed, but left that impression. Don Antonio Peralta died on his way to California in 1865. Don Antonio was over 90 years of age at the time of his death. None of the friends of the Peraltas accompanied Miguel to work the mine in the Superstition Mountains.

NOTES—Continued

Doc. Willing is often confused with Jack Swilling, a well-known pioneer in Arizona.

The Peralta land grant originated by Don Antonio was a fraud. J. A. Reavis, erstwhile street car conductor, and lawyer of sorts, tried to prove the authenticity of the Peralta claim by changing the records in California, Mexico, Cuba and Spain. Reavis tried to prove that his wife, the daughter of a Digger Indian Squaw and a white man, was the only remaining descendant of the Peralta family. The Peralta family of Spain, according to Reavis, had been extinct for more than a hundred years. He also said the Peraltas in this country were and are descendants of servants of the Peralta family of Spain.

Don Antonio and Don Miguel were self-styled Dons and not Dons by birth or accomplishments.

The location of the mine is in the Superstition Range of Mountains south of the Rio Salado or Salt River. Many people are of the opinion that the mine is north of the Salt River. I am afraid these people have their mines twisted. There are other mines discovered by Dutchmen north of the Salt River, but the Lost Dutchman Mine is south. Every German was called a Dutchman and that is the reason for so many varied tales.

The following lost mines were discovered by Dutchmen and are erroneously called Lost Dutchman: The

NOTES—Continued

Dr. Thorne Mine, The Adam's Diggings, and The Lost Shoemaker Placer.

There is also confusion, in the minds of those who think they know all about the Lost Dutchman, concerning the name of the man or men who started the story.

Jacob Walz and Jacob Wiser were the names of the two men. These two men are well authenticated. There are some few old-timers left who remember them and the beginning of the tale of the Lost Dutchman Mine. These men are about equally divided in their opinion of the existence or non-existence of the mine.

These men are not the original men of the Lost Dutchman: Frank Ricken (real name) or Frank Branden (assumed name), Paul Ludy or Jacobs of one story, Jack Swartz, Andy Starr or a man whose last name was Jacob.

Jacob Walz did not tell J. R. Holmes any tale about the mine, nor did Holmes get any $500 or more in gold rock from under the bed of the Dutchman, because Walz was dead before Holmes came to Arizona.

There is one and possibly two authentic maps of the mine in existence. One of these fits the written tale of Ballesteros like a glove, also the weeded dope of Walz. The other map is in the possession of a man who will not let anyone see it, but from information gathered it must be a copy of the one already viewed.

DIFFERENT WAYS TO FIND PRECIOUS METALS

Thousands of men and women are prospecting "rather blindly" for gold and other precious metals. Here are a few simple, mind's-eye ways of improving on this "blindness," covering all the old prospector's tricks and the most up-to-date scientific methods of prospecting:

Roots of trees uprotted by the winds sometimes expose ores and mineral outcrops. The rich Mesabe Range in Minnesota was discovered by observing hematite in the roots of a tree at Biwabik, in 1891.

The famous Potosi (Bolivia) silver mines developed from noticing silver in the roots of a bush pulled out accidentally by a native.

Pronounced differences in trees and plants are sometimes caused by the kind of underlying bed rock.

Heavy growths of trees, such as aspens, or the presence of plants requiring much water, may indicate fissured areas underneath favorable to mineralization.

Contrast in color may occur between vegetation over a mineral outcrop, and that around it. An airplane shows this plainly, though it may not be noticed by men on the ground.

In regions of sulphide ores or minerals, trees are likely to be sickly and quite stunted by injurious gases.

Sometimes the melting of snow over certain areas indicates heat rising from below from oxidation of sulphides, arsenides and, rarely, of copper. Freedom from frost is another "sign" of such treasure areas.

Burrowing animals and birds have brought to man the first news of many of our large mines. Pellets of gold in crops of game birds have been traced to their source through knowledge of the birds' feeding habits.

The first trace of copper in South Australia was green material found near a wombat hole in 1860.

Gold in the crop of a domestic turkey led to the latest gold field of the State of Washington.

Fires have melted sulphides of silver leaving the silver exposed to view. Thus the shining objects in a camp fire near Catorce, Mexico, in 1775, led to mining $200,000,000 worth of silver in that vicinity.

A line of springs may indicate a "fault" or a vein below. Geysers indicate sulphur by fumes or hydrogen sulphide.

Numerous paying mines have been located through ancient, abandoned workings such as pits, trenches, or slag heaps. Wars, floods or other causes have led to abandonment with rich minerals still there.

The Rio Grande Press, Inc.

GLORIETA, NEW MEXICO · 87535

BASIC SOURCE BOOKS OF AMERICAN HISTORY

64-20401
Amsden, Charles Avery
Navaho Weaving its Technic and History $12.00

78-76176
Audubon, John Woodhouse
The Western Journals, Mexico/California 1849-1850 ...... $ 8.00

64-15127
Bartlett, John Russell
A Personal Narrative of Explorations $32.50

62-17903
Bourke, John Gregory
On the Border with Crook; new edition, new index ...... $ 9.00

62-21941
Bourke, John Gregory
Snake Dance of the Moqui (Hopi) Indians .... $ 8.00

65-20151
Brooks, Nathan Covington
A Complete History of the Mexican War $17.50

78-85496
Coyner, David H.
The Lost Trappers; an Account of the Fur Trade ...... $ 8.00

72-81809
Cremony, John C.
Life Among the Apaches $10.00

68-31292
Jocknick, Sidney
Early Days on the Western Slope of Colorado ...... $ 8.00

66-26008
Jones, Anson
Republic of Texas, its History and Annexation $25.00

67-26680
Kluckhohn, Clyde
To the Foot of the Rainbow .... $ 7.00

62-20277
Kubler, George
Religious Architecture of New Mexico $12.00

37-15022
McKenna, James A.
Black Range Tales .... $ 7.50

68-25390
Reichard, Gladys A.
Navajo Shepherd and Weaver .... $ 8.00

68-25391
Reichard, Gladys A.
Spider Woman: Life Among the Navajo .... $ 8.00

63-21232
Sedgwick, Mrs. W. T.
Acoma, the Sky City .... $ 7.50

62-17905
Dellenbaugh, Frederick S.
The Romance of the Colorado River .... $ 7.50

63-21229
Falconer, Thomas
Texan-Santa Fe Expedition .... $ 7.00

62-20282
Fewkes, Jesse Walter
Hopi Katcinas Drawn by Native Artists $15.00

62-17906
Forrest, Earle R.
Missions and Pueblos of the Old Southwest .... $ 7.50

77-81810
Hilzinger, J. George
Treasure Land; a Handbook to Southern Arizona 1897 ... $ 7.00

71-76177
Hobbs, Capt. James
Wild Life in the Far West 1840-1870 .... $12.00

62-17907
Hodge, Hiram C.
Arizona as it Was, 1877 .... $ 7.00

62-20279
Hughes, John T.
Doniphan's Expedition, 1846-1848 .... $ 8.00

67-30871
Ide, William B.; Ide, Simeon
Who Conquered California? $10.00

75-76178
Ingersoll, Ernest
Crest of the Continent; Railroad Rambles in the Rockies
1885; the Narrow Gauge in Colo., N. M., & Utah ...... $ 8.00

Shea, John Gilmary
The Expedition of Dionisio de Penalosa .... $ 7.00

62-20280
Sitgreaves, Lorenzo
Report of an Expedition down the Zuni .... $ 8.00

67-26678
Taylor, Bayard
Eldorado, or, Adventures in the Path of Empire $12.00

63-21233
Twitchell, Ralph Emerson
The Military Occupation of New Mexico .... $ 8.50

63-21234
Twitchell, Ralph Emerson
Old Sante Fe $12.00

62-17908
Villagra, Gaspar de
A History of New Mexico .... $ 8.00

68-25392
Walters, Lorenzo D.
Tombstone's Yesterday: Bad Men of Arizona .... $ 7.50

68-25393
Wharton, Clarence Ray
Remember Goliad; A Rollcall of Texas Heroes .... $ 7.00

64-15130
Winship, George Parker
The Coronado Expedition, 1540-1542 .... $17.50

71-79684
Wislizenus, Frederick Adolph
Journey to the Rocky Mountains 1839 .... $10.00

74-85495
Wislizenus, Frederick Adolph
Tour to Northern Mexico with Col. Doniphan 1846-1847 .. $10.00

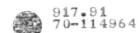